822.33
/ BER

D1150355

MMT

I AM HAMLET

by the same author

WEST AND OTHER PLAYS
KVETCH/ACAPULCO
SINK THE BELGRANO!
DECADENCE AND OTHER PLAYS

I AM HAMLET

Steven Berkoff

faber and faber
LONDON·BOSTON

First published in Great Britain in 1989
by Faber and Faber Limited
3 Queen Square London WC1N 3AU

Photoset by Wilmaset, Birkenhead, Wirral
Printed in Great Britain by
Richard Clay Ltd, Bungay, Suffolk

A CIP record for this book is available from the British Library.

ISBN 0-571-15279-1

All quotations from *Hamlet* are taken from the Arden edition,
published by Methuen and Co. Ltd.

Olio/92

INTRODUCTION

In every actor is a Hamlet struggling to get out. In fact, in most directors too.

For whatever reason, and there are many, Hamlet is the accumulation of all our values and beliefs. In him are set out the rules for the perfect human, the perfect rationalist, plus the adventurer, all rolled into one. No other play gives an actor such words of compassion, charm, wisdom, wit, moral force, insight, and philosophy.

The actor needs to feel those things within his own breast and to touch these words is to set alight a small flame within himself. We all wish to be . . . Hamlet and cast our torch over the iniquities and sins of others as he does now and will do in the future, and in all times and in all styles.

Hamlet is a feast for the actor since there is something naturally of Hamlet in us all . . . there is maybe one speech that will touch one actor more than another, one scene that fits so like a glove while another does not. Since Hamlet touches the complete alphabet of human experience every actor feels he is born to play it.

The bold extrovert will dazzle and play with the word power, the scenes of vengeance, and blast Ophelia and Gertrude off the stage. The introvert will see every line pointed at him, the outsider, the loner, the watcher, he, with his one trusting friend, and a quick answer for everything lest it be a barb. The wit will play for laughs and the lunatic for madness. The romantic for ideals. So you cannot be miscast for Hamlet – '*fatally* miscast' as one critic called me in fact – since he too had *his* version of Hamlet fixed in his head.

Hamlet doesn't exist as Macbeth or Coriolanus or Romeo exists. The actions of these creatures determine who they are and even what they look like. They are led by forces which shape them. Hamlet is not led by anything. He reacts to everything. He is of all things an opinion. A quest for the most perfect we can make ourselves. So I *am*

Hamlet since when you *play* Hamlet he becomes *you*. When you play Hamlet, you play yourself and play the instrument which is you. If you can make a good tune as an actor your best tunes will come out of Hamlet and if not then that does not matter but you will be a better actor for having played it, and been there.

So one day I decided to put all fears and doubts to one side and get on with it.

In order to play Hamlet I felt I had to direct it since I might wait for ever otherwise and I had fancied the play for many years as an actor and director. The first and usual fear besetting actor/directors is how to imbue the cast with a faith in their ability to do both tasks. If I faltered would their faith in me, and their resolve in the play, weaken? How to start? I always look for a sign or a kernel round which to build. What is the clue?

To strengthen my courage I worked alone in a studio in Edinburgh, encouraged by my old partner Shelley Lee. I ventured into the empty space and placed a chair in the middle of the room. Claudius was the chair and praying, and I approached him:

Now might I do it pat, now a is a-praying.

The words soared into my skull and caught fire and I felt that tingle of excitement that every performer knows when he has ignited his adrenalin and believes he is on the way.

I wanted the actors to remain on stage with me the whole time as if they were witnesses at a trial. It was to be a dissection of the play with the actors as observers watching and reflecting and ready to be called to give their evidence. I wanted no central star around which other satellites revolved, lit up for a brief moment in the star's glow and then cast into the wintry outlands of a dressing room for endless hours. We had to be in it together, part of the fabric of the play. I, as Hamlet, in fact wanted to see what they were doing at any given moment.

The play was eventually to be performed in the round or the square and was destined for the Round House, that majestic temple of the most arcane in Chalk Farm. I liked the Round House and had made it my sanctuary on two occasions in the past when George Hoskins had made me feel not only welcome but positively wanted and I loved him for it. He brought to that eerie old engine-shed some of the most exciting theatre ever to be seen and his exit began the slide that was to end in its eventual demise as a theatrical venue. Its very location, atmosphere, and even its bar, made it a place to go as an alternative to the grim and tight West End.

We started with three actors in rehearsal and then added one or two at a time as I worked out a scheme and sketched ideas with my lieutenants Matthew Scurfield and Barry Philips, who were, with me, the architects of the style the production would have. Eventually we performed the play with ten people.

It began life in Edinburgh in August 1979 and continued in 1980 at the Round House, where we received the most awful battering from the press. Undeterred we played it in Europe for the next two years and completed the final performance as guests of Jean-Louis Barrault at his Rond Point Théâtre (strange coincidence), where the audience got to their feet and gave us one of the most moving ovations we had yet heard. Whether the production had improved or not since the Round House, the critical reactions on the Continent could not have been further removed from the English response. You would have thought they were not writing about the same production.

We toured throughout Europe, avoiding England, and found wherever we went a most earnest and enthusiastic reception. Critically the play was well received in Israel, Holland, Belgium, Germany, and most of all in France. Thank God for Europe and for the impresario Jan de Bleik who brought us there, for without Europe we would have been a sorry experiment that failed. We were able to perform, develop, grow into our roles and become a company, and of course earn wages.

During the tour I started to keep a journal and record the workings of the play from a director/actor's point of view. I wanted to show a line by line examination of the text and how we dealt with it in terms of the production, so in effect what follows is a production diary. It was a fascinating task for me but I was able to do it only on tour when the early breakfasts in some small German town fuelled me to remain at the table with hot strong coffee and write. I had the performances in the evening and apart from the journey the day was mine.

I liked writing it and I hope it conveys a bird's-eye view of the working of *Hamlet*. I call it *I Am Hamlet* since I am looking at the proceedings with the eye of an actor, and partly because whoever plays Hamlet *is* Hamlet. Being now Hamlet I felt I could comment on what was around me from his point of view. It has been a pleasure to write and I hope it will be a pleasure to read. In all, this journal took probably two years to put together and may be a guide to a journey I, and nine people, made ten years ago.

S.B.

Dedicated to all who journeyed with me and made this possible.

Actors
Barry Philips
Matthew Scurfield
Linda Marlowe
Chloë Salaman
Gary Whelan
Rory Edwards
Bob Hornery
Wolf Kahler
David Meyer
Tony Meyer
Sally Bentley
Terry McGinity
Nigel Williams
David Auker
Roy

Encouragement
Jan de Bleik (Holland)
Avatal Mossinson (Israel)
Jean-Louis Barrault (France)
Joanna Marston (Britain)

Music
John Prior

Photographer
Roger Morton

Valuable Assistants
Deborah Warner
Howard Harrison
Perdita Kark

ACT I

I am Hamlet.

Ten people walk in. They are in dress suits – black and white. The playing area is a square tending to a rectangle. There are lines across and on the diagonal, plus a circle in the centre. These areas are demarcated by white tape. It looks like a playing field or basketball court – or areas of the brain. In this case it is like a ground plan of a castle before the walls are constructed: walkways, battlements, etc. The walls are invisible and two actors will pass without seeing each other. There is an imaginary wall in between. Forty chairs line the four sides to be accessible at all times. The actors play all the thirty or so characters. There are ten of them. They sit in the chairs and wait to go on. While waiting they are part of the scene. They change like chameleons, or sometimes become a mirror for the events in the centre. When they are sitting the audience is able to examine them. They are neutral observers, sometimes staying within their characters but often returning, not as passive observers, but as people caught within the environment – as in religious paintings where the subsidiary figures enhance the whole by focusing on the centre. Occasionally they will express a reverse view and wish to hide their faces or block their ears at talk of conspiracy, or be a satirical counterpoint to it.

The actors march on, and sit. The audience identifies Hamlet, who is wearing a double-breasted suit, black shirt and tie. He sits next to Ophelia and holds her hand. They are seated in a line and are quite still. A musician cracks a drum and the house lights go out. The audience jumps at the sound and then giggles foolishly.

SCENE I

We hear the wind tearing round the turrets. It is the breath of the actors. They make the wind. They act as orchestra, both physically and psychically. Two men rise and approach each other on the diagonal from opposite sides. They walk very slowly and carefully, as in a mist. One is Barnardo, come to relieve his companion on the watch. It's cold. They wear their collars up. A shout stuns the air. The first line:

Barnardo **Who's there?**

It's a thunderclap – sudden, frightening, and the front rows again start in their seats.

Francisco **Nay, answer me. Stand and unfold yourself.**

The shout's force removes the ball of fear that has lodged in his throat. He is frightened in case the ghost materializes. We hear Horatio joined by Marcellus. He has left the ranks of the actors and runs with Marcellus the entire perimeter of the stage. They run in perfect military unison like Sandhurst cadets. We see them run up imaginary stairs to the platform, and by their movements are able to see the structure of the castle at this point. The castle's shape needs to be defined since we are using an empty square. We can make of it what we will; our moves determine the rooms and corridors. The two men greet with enthusiasm and recount the story:

Barnardo **Last night of all,**
When yond same star that's westward from the pole,
Had made his course t'illumine that part of heaven
Where now it burns, Marcellus and myself,
The bell then beating one –

Nice crisp, cold sounds like *star* and *pole*, and evidence of time and place. Barnardo could be giving evidence in court.

From the chorus of players the Ghost has unpeeled himself and begins his slow, ponderous walk, as if clad in marble, his jaw thrust

4

out, calmly making his nightly perambulation. He bisects the stage along the diagonal. The three men throw themselves back against the invisible fourth wall and plaster themselves on it while the Ghost moves as if drawn by invisible wires. The effect is hypnotic since he cannot stop walking and is doomed to walk in perpetuity. His steady walk suggests that he has already walked for thousands upon thousands of fruitless, silent miles. Just walking as if there is no end and nothing to be gained except more walking:

Ghost **Doom'd for a certain term to walk the night,**
And for the day confin'd to fast in fires . . . [I, v]

I wondered why the spirit of the dead king would be made to suffer unendurably in fire when he was innocent of any crime. Somebody actually murdered him. And he is made to suffer not only pain in loss of life but a second pain in torment because the crime done to him has not been purged. Absurd proposition. Why should he who was

the front of Jove himself

. . .

Where every god did seem to set his seal
To give the world assurance of a man [III, iv]

be suffering a torment in hell-like purgatory . . . because he was killed without the benefit of confession of which a dying man may have the chance to avail himself. So the chance death without leaving a forgive-me note condemns him for ever. It is a cruelty that only the fifteenth-century Catholic church could dream up.

He crosses the stage and disappears into the chorus again. They try to draw conclusions and discover if the appearance is in anger or an omen. Horatio first analyses the political events and fills in a little background for the audience. And then, just as abruptly, the Ghost leaves. We cut this to the essential. Just enough for the information. Having bored and confused everybody politically, Horatio discusses phychic phenomena as harbingers of disquiet, with ridiculous images of the dead wrapped in bed sheets and squeaking. Naturally we left this out. The Ghost re-enters on *preparations*. He commences his walk again. Shakespeare needed time for Horatio and the soldiers to talk and for the audience to forget about the Ghost for its return to be

5

effective. What Horatio says is misleading since the Ghost is not returning as a harbinger of bad tidings. This information can befuddle the audience, since at this stage of the game they pay rapt attention to the plot because they are witnessing 'Shakespeare'; they feel that anything they miss will be like dropping some valuable thread which plays a vital part in the grand design. So cut it. Shakespeare has a habit at the beginning of plays of being like a frantic knitter with four needles and many colours. He digresses and needs trimming to reveal the core.

The orchestra takes up the sound of the Ghost. Low hum: almost a Buddhist chant. It's deep in the throat, a sound that could be hammy in the wrong hands – just a texture, almost to let us know that he is coming before he is seen. This becomes most effective when the sound stops and the chorus resumes the wind sound.

Now the humming resumes as if the Ghost were carrying his own inferno with him. Horatio kneels as the Ghost passes him, but not in the path of the Ghost. Since Horatio cannot summon the spirit to speak he attacks it and they all lunge and strike with their invisible weapons.

But the Ghost continues and they strike at space. They spin around in quick movements: careful, nervous and watchful.

Marcellus reflects on the stupidity of violence which Horatio was quite out of character in suggesting:

> Marcellus **We do it wrong, being so majestical,**
> **To offer it the show of violence** . . .

To make up for his apparent loss of philosophical judgement Horatio enters into another peregrination, which is followed by the simple statement:

> Marcellus **It faded on the crowing of the cock.**

But then Marcellus starts waxing poetic and further confuses the issue so we stopped his mouth on *It faded on the crowing of the cock*. We leave the scene with Horatio wrapping up the night in verse which is descriptive and of value. Shakespeare likes to announce the time and space.

6

SCENE II

The council chamber in the castle.

The three players turning slowly as they follow Horatio's last speech merge with the chorus and take their chairs to the centre. As this is happening we hear the first birds of dawn, and then this fades to leave us with a grand circle in the middle. We imagine a huge table in the centre. It is a council meeting. I take my chair and place it nearly opposite Claudius and facing Gertrude. On my right sits Laertes and next to him Polonius. The rest of the cast forms the circle. Since we are not bound by any convention to remain with our one character but slip briefly into others, Ophelia is now the court stenographer and is taking notes.

The economy of playing other roles comes less from financial needs than from the idea that ten people can easily flow through other roles as required. To burden the stage with bodies is both unimaginative and wasteful. It is wasteful in terms of human energy and also clutters the course of the play. We are after all telling a story and if there is labour available then Laertes, Horatio and Rosencrantz quite easily double in the opening scene. This stretches the skills of the actors and intensifies the playing energy, rather than having able-bodied players sitting in a dressing room for hours waiting for an entrance.

So I am awaiting the first moment when I am to speak. The King raises his hand and the hubbub of the court stops. Claudius clears his throat and begins. He stands above his chair, gripping the back. Gertrude looks at me and I avoid her glance. She is wearing a black, tight-fitting skirt which reveals a generous wodge of thigh, and wears around her shoulders a fur piece or feather boa; on her head a black hat with a small black lace veil. She is well made-up with a bright red mouth. Claudius is bald, shaved to the skull, looking quite mephisto-phelean, and wears a tail suit and wing collar. He has a booming voice. I am wearing a striped double-breasted suit which is almost black and looks as if it was made in the forties. It fits well and feels good. He commences. It is the familiar whitewash speech. From time to time the group claps some little nicety.

7

King **For all, our thanks.**

He is in a good mood and inclined to lend an ear to pleas, bolstering the nationalistic spirit with a bit of sabre rattling. He risks a little theatricality as well by a contemptuous spit on *So much for him*, referring to young Fortinbras's design on some lands that are in dispute. The group laughs and claps the audacious gesture. Claudius is going down well. Laertes rises, egged on by his dad, and makes his little speech about wishing to get back to France. I shouldn't wonder after dreary Elsinore. Polonius gets up and down, and now it is on Hamlet that the searchlight is directed.

There is something dreadfully disquieting about waiting to say your first speech. You hear everyone speaking over you like voices disembodied or in a dream. You can hardly pay too much attention to what else is going on but you try, if only to direct the energy away from yourself, for it is liable to attack and inflame your fears. You may find yourself thinking about the first line and suddenly you are not on that speeding train, you have got off. You shake the words away and look at Gertrude and Claudius and feed your inner computer with instructions of bile, hate and revenge. But your first speech is flying towards you. The energy pumps blood at a greater speed and now I sense a tickle in my throat; I want to discharge it and softly clear it using Claudius's speech as my cover. But the tickle remains and now it seems my throat is covered in molasses. In the dressing room it was like a cutting edge but now I am a sprinter in glue. I open my mouth and breathe slowly but the fish are there swimming with fins inside the cords that are my instrument. The only way I can get it out is to squeeze it out through the nose.

It's coming closer . . . the dread moment. The audience grows silent. They want to hear how the 'title' of the play sounds. They are almost afraid of him. He is mythologized in their deepest unconscious and everyone in the world knows some of his lines. He is almost unreal. A figment of their ancient schoolchild past. He is also their hero; the reason for coming out on a wet night. This is the reason: you. Me. They are waiting for you to open your mouth and make them thrill to the sound that defies all opposition. A voice that pales

8

the other. An honesty that exposes by its sheer clarity the others . . . the bosses and the liars, the dishonest politicians, the scoundrels, the murderers and schemers. As he is their Hamlet, so he is their conscience too. His cause is the cause of the audience for they are also idealists. Hamlet is our better self and we want to see how he can save us by not compromising. So all eyes focus on me. Claudius gives a lilt to his speech in relief knowing that his peroration is coming to an end and, having had a good warm up, he gloats since he now hands over the reins to me.

I have been playing 'cool', one leg crossed over, or rather the ankle resting on one knee. Slumped in indifference, my hands thrust in my jacket pockets as if I wanted to escape inside myself and all I could get in was my hands.

King **But now, my cousin Hamlet, and my son –**
I try to be as clear as I can but the voice is a squeak. It has been frozen into impotence by the wait. I try to put some significance into –

Hamlet **A little more than kin, and less than kind.**
It is really an aside that Claudius pretends not to hear, yet at the same time waits for – one of those annoying asides, half meant for his ears. But it is an aside since I break into his speech before he can finish. I reply that I am too much in the sun (son) – oh yeah, ha ha ha.

So here in the beginning Hamlet is showing his wit, sending the old codgers up with a display of coarse wit that clothes his disgust. Claudius is an unpopular uncle who probably pinched Hamlet's bum when he was little and tweaked his hair. But now he is in my place; not only King Hamlet's but the place of young Hamlet who should have been asked to take over the reins. Gertrude speaks and I reply:

Hamlet **Ay, madam, it is common.**
The voice is beginning to return to home having fled in fear. Now, seeing that the words are actually coming out, the energy is returning to support the field.

Seems, madam?
I like this and jump on it . . . 'seems??? madam . . . Nay, it *IS*' . . . or, 'seems?? *MADAM*!' as if *MADAM* how dare you . . . or are you

really such a madam? I rise since everyone else has and talk to the assembly . . . give them all a piece and watch them squirm in discomfort –

Nor customary suits . . .

– fastening my eyes on *them*. They are capable of show . . . *forc'd breath, fruitful river* – all these addresses are to each of them and lay the charge of hypocrisy on all of them. Lovely. I watch them shift in discomfort and turn away. I am taking it easy, not too important – more like an afterthought. I prepare to sit on *which passes show* and have started my descent when, to put the twist in, I rise again, but not quite to my full height, and explain,

These but the trappings and the suits of woe.

My suit, mate, like yours, is outward mourning. Heh, heh . . .

There's a little sputter of coughing now and a few curdled looks in my direction, particularly from Laertes, the good boy with his unctuous, toe-licking speech. Claudius continues attempting to wash away any trace of bile by going into the attack, honeying his first words to give credence to his later ones, which imply there's something whinging about being in grief for a mere few weeks. And then dropping hints that I am somehow immediate to the throne – as if any minute now he will abdicate – and then ending with a great mouthful of Cs: *cheer, comfort, chiefest, courtier* and *cousin*. Phew! I think he was trying to say 'You c—!' but his finale earns rounds of applause from the court as if to confirm his speech had effectively washed away any bad taste or smell in the air.

The Queen now mouths something motherly about not going:

Queen . . . **Go not to Wittenberg.**

Ah, I look at my watch . . . it's a bit of a rush for the last train, thus neatly implying that the only thing that would keep me in this bleak dungeon would be lack of transport. (Laughter from audience. They appreciate the insult.)

Hamlet **I shall in all my best obey you, madam.**

The King repeats how loving I am and goes:

King **Come away.**

HAMLET HAS DEMONSTRATED HIS POWER BY SHOWING COMPLETE
DISREGARD FOR THE ETIQUETTE OF COURT OR OF KEEPING YOUR
MOUTH SHUT. IN DOING SO HE HAS UNDERMINED CLAUDIUS'S
POSITION SIMPLY AND WITH EASE WHILE CLAUDIUS HAS
ATTEMPTED TO SUBORDINATE HIM WITH EPITHETS LIKE *sweet,
loving, gentle, unforced.* LATER HAMLET WILL SAY,

break, my heart, for I must hold my tongue

BUT IT WOULD BE EASIER TO HOLD A SNAKE. HAMLET CANNOT
HOLD HIS TONGUE. HIS IS THE MIND THAT CANNOT HELP BUT
RESPOND WHEN BANALITIES ARE BEING HEAPED ON IT. HE IS
EXACT AND WILL PROD UNTIL THE TRUTH IS REVEALED. THAT'S
WHAT HE IS SUPPOSED TO BE DOING IN WITTENBERG: STUDYING
PHILOSOPHY. HE DEMANDS EXACTNESS AND DIRECTNESS AND
ANYTHING ELSE IS A SLACK LINE FOR THIS PARTICULAR TIGHT-
ROPE-WALKER. UNACCUSTOMED AS WE ARE TO SAYING WHAT WE
THINK AND FEEL, WE ENGINEER LOTS OF SILLY GAMES AND
CONFUSING MANOEUVRES TO ENABLE US TO TURN THE WIT TO
OUR ADVANTAGE. HAMLET'S MIND IS A MIRROR THAT REFLECTS
THE TRUTH UNDER THE GARISH MAKE-UP AND IT IS A MIRROR
THAT ONLY THE STRONG OR THE HONEST WILL WANT TO GAZE AT.
HE X-RAYS YOUR HEART. IT IS NOT A COMFORTABLE EXPERIENCE
TO BE WITH HIM. ON THE OTHER HAND IT CAN BE EXHILARATING
IF YOU LIKE HEIGHTS. WHY WE IDENTIFY WITH HIM IS FOR THIS
REASON: THAT HE WILL SPEAK HIS MIND WHILE WE CRINGE WHEN
THE OPPORTUNITY PRESENTS ITSELF TO FELL SOME SMALL,
FOETID LITTLE DRAGON. WE TURN AWAY WHILE HE FACES IT. HE
SPEAKS THE THINGS WE WOULD LIKE TO. WE WILL PURGE
OURSELVES THROUGH HIS BLOOD.

King **Come away.**

The first time we did this we kept the chorus in a frozen state in their
chairs: a photograph just as they were about to leave, turning in their
seats, leaning forward.

Hamlet **O** . . .

I howl it out. At last they are gone but the chorus is there as a fresco in my mind's eye and now I will use it as I circle the stage. I am alone.

O . . .

I could scream – or cry with frustration. I get up and walk slowly round the interior of the circle. I did not see this as a reflective speech with Hamlet left on the shore of his introspection as the court goes out like a great tide of scum, leaving him to make his speech. Nor the usual seated prince with one leg crossed over the ankle in self-pitying *Angst* and plot plot plot. I walk and survey them.

two months . . . nay, not so much, not two –

Or is it twice two months . . . who knows? Time goes fast in this play. I am alone. I could scream. How dare he?

married with my uncle

There he is in the chair, i.e. in my mind's eye. I walk around and survey them and her:

might not beteem the winds of heaven
Visit her face too roughly.
. . . Frailty, thy name is woman.

This to Ophelia. All there conveniently sitting in the frame of my mind's eye. So it becomes almost a lecture to the audience; like an examination of police photographs.

I have to keep moving, albeit slowly, savouring the words. Calm as ice; the scream has been let out. They look like exhibits in Tussaud's Chamber of Horrors. Sometimes past I have sat here in my room in London and surveyed the doom-laden greyness and felt it would be better to be dead than this.

O that this too too sullied flesh would melt,
Thaw and resolve itself into a dew . . .

I confess to the audience my pain and the reasons . . . my body a wrack of pain with the text breaking over me in waves . . .

'tis an unweeded garden
That grows to seed; things rank and gross in nature
Possess it merely.

My hand is open and imagines something living in it, and then it closes and crushes it. I relive the horror, retasting the bile to keep my

spleen recharged . . . *But two months dead . . . nay, not so much . . .*
So excellent a king . . . Visit her face too roughly – almost touching my
mother and letting my hand flutter down as if sculpting with it. I taste
and relish the event while saying,

Must I remember?

He not only remembers but keeps sucking at the memory for some
new flavours. My words cut through the air, not dragged out but clear
and succinct, as if hung on the air or given in evidence. But emotion
now could cloud the text. So observe . . .

or ere those shoes were old

How did she look?

Like Niobe, all tears . . .

O God, a beast that wants discourse of reason
Would have mourn'd longer –

Not human but *a beast*. I hit the last line as a summation of the speech
up to now . . . a beast . . . even a *beast*! How pathetic . . . a dumb,
stupid animal would have the right instincts.

My journey takes me round the circle to Claudius . . .

. . . married with my uncle,
My father's brother – but no more like my father
Than I to Hercules.

Sitting there in my mind's eye – this object of disgust . . . not even
horror, but amazement. To place him in my father's bed! To have
him as a father . . . *My cousin Hamlet, and my son.* When a father
should be the perfection of malehood. Fathers are gods, immortal and
flawless. Since they were there when we first opened our eyes on the
world, they and our mothers are the first pillars of our universe – we
cannot fault them since we are babes. Father and mother are man and
wife. They are one flesh and the son is part of that triad of flesh. Now
Claudius has invaded that sanctuary and thus invades Hamlet's own
body.

Within a month,
Ere yet the salt of most unrighteous tears
Had left the flushing in her galled eyes,
She married . . .

The hit. She married. The climax of all – unbelievable . . . don't the jury think this is astonishing? *She married.*

O most wicked speed!

Drop the voice . . . a little *sotto voce* . . . with two drops of vinegar on *wicked* . . . a touch of wickedness driving the motors there, what?

To post

With such dexterity to incestuous sheets!

Sheetssss! A mouthful of *ssss*. A basket of snakes. On the *s* hang vicious, lewd, sex-stained sheets.

But break, my heart, for I must hold my tongue.

The whole speech is almost a voice-over in his mind as the King is speaking. In a film I would have the whole speech as voice-over while the King makes his opening speech. I would feed it between the pauses.

King **Come away**.

The waxworks come to life as if the whole speech has been thought out in his head.

I did this play one year later and changed this completely. I have always felt a pang of guilt in allowing players to be just figures while I am able to record off them, so to speak, although the frozen figures were not the hanging-around figures that grace most of the Shakespearian productions that we see – those slack and vague lumps that pretend to be in conversation while the actor races through his soliloquy. The fresco was already a powerful image but I had the notion that the actors would be better exploited as living performers if they were in fact moving throughout the scene and saying farewell to Hamlet, patting him on the back in consolation, shaking hands, kissing his mother and generally doing all that protocol demands. Now during this movement I timed the (silent) goodbyes to coincide with the text, so I would be saying *married with my uncle* while actually shaking hands with him. And *Frailty, thy name is woman* neatly occurred as I was kissing Ophelia's hand. The effect was startling and gave the actors an involvement with the scene that required just about perfect timing. As they leave Horatio is just another figure that I shake hands with. I have finished the speech. It's early in the play and one cannot do more than draw the audience into the area . . . entice them in trippingly on the tongue and not blast off and exhaust them and yourself too early. In some way, one is analysing Hamlet by a process of surgical operation, and so the operation is on myself. We are holding up the specimen and unpeeling a nerve here and there.

Horatio   **Hail to your lordship**.

He has been sitting there all the time. I did not see him. I was too wrapped up in myself. All the court (chorus) have left, centre stage.

Hamlet   **I am glad to see you well**.

(Sudden realization) 'Horatio!! Or do I forget myself.' This reading is much favoured by the slightly slow-witted Hamlet who breaks off in the middle suddenly to realize a friend is here, and one has to suffer this punishing cliché – especially in our Shakespeare Emporiums which seldom offer up anything new but rather regurgitate the old and well worn. Shakespeare is seldom equivocal. When he starts a line he is not playing naturalistic tricks. The line is:

I am glad to see you well.

Horatio, or do I forget myself.

Which palpably means, 'I would rather forget who I am than not see and hope thee well,' and not, 'Oh my God, dear boy, I didn't recognize you for a moment.' Nor is Hamlet the hypocrite to say, 'I am glad to see you well' to a stranger.

THIS FONDNESS FOR NATURALISTIC GESTURES HAS AFFORDED US SOME AWFUL *HAMLET*S AND I HAVE SEEN THE WORST. THE VERY WORST. THE MOST WORST. THE UTMOST, BORING, UNCUT VERSIONS – AS IF THERE WAS SOMETHING VIRTUOUS AND NOURISHING ABOUT AN UNCUT *HAMLET*. ALL IT DOES IS TO REVEAL THE IMBECILITY OF THE DIRECTOR AND CAST AND MAKES FOR A BAD EVENING, SINCE THE UNCUTTING IMPLIES A WHOLLY INGRATIATING ATTITUDE WHICH WILL IMPEDE ANY REAL INSIGHTS (I.E. CHALLENGE, LIFE, LIGHT, IMAGINATION) INTO THE PLAY. TWO DEATHLY PRODUCTIONS IN PARTICULAR WERE DISTINGUISHED BY THE FACT THAT IT WAS THE SAME DIRECTOR WHO INFLICTED

THEM ON US WITH A TEN-YEAR INTERVAL. THEY WERE WHAT YOU MIGHT CALL ANTI-HAMLET, BECAUSE IF THERE WAS A VERB 'TO HAMLET' IT WOULD MEAN TO PUNCTURE, TO RENDER STUPID BY EXPOSING, TO ILLUMINATE. IF EVER I SAW A MIND THAT MATCHED THE WIT AND QUICKNESS OF HAMLET'S, IT WAS OLIVIER'S. TO PLAY GENIUS AND EVEN DIRECT IT ONE SHOULD BE MAKING A MARRIAGE LEST THE NATURE OF ONE GENIUS EXPOSE THE OTHER'S LACK OF IT. TWO EQUAL PARTNERS MATE, SPAR, FIGHT, DANCE, COPULATE AND WATCH THE SPARKS FLY, BUT LET ONE BE DULLER THAN THE OTHER AND DULLER BY FAR, THEN WE ARE AFFORDED THE SPECTACLE OF A LOATHSOME PIECE OF LARD MADE EVEN MORE SO BY THE VERY INEPTITUDE OF THE OPERATION. TO OPERATE ON HAMLET YOU SHOULD BE A BRAIN SURGEON, NOT A BUTCHER.

Hamlet   **I am glad to see you well**

   . . .

      And what make you from Wittenberg . . . ?

The cast has sat and occupies two sides of the stage. *What make you from Wittenberg?* Is it possible that Hamlet doesn't know and didn't see him at the wedding or the funeral? And if the funeral was less than two months ago, has Horatio been hanging around and waiting for the wedding before announcing himself? These things don't matter. It is there for the contrast of the two events to be reiterated and to introduce Horatio. I suppose the university was so big he didn't catch Hamlet during lunch recess to say, 'Oh, by the way, old chap, I'm going to your dad's funeral.' And yet they are supposed to be the most loyal friends. But there you go. It doesn't pay to analyse the events in the play since it isn't real. It is the ideas that are real. Gary Whelan plays Horatio. He stands straight in a smart double-breasted suit and looks as if he could shift a few troublesome fellows out of a bar if need be. Why should he look like a drip? Many very sturdy fellows have been known to go to public school and make formidable rugger players – even boxers – so I throw a punch and he blocks it in the

16

familiar way mates do, pretending to catch their chum off guard with a feigned left hook. It's an automatic response. It shows in a quick gesture, a symbol of loyalty. You shake your enemy's hand politely. Marcellus and Barnardo are also waiting at the entrance of the circle which seems curious if this is an informal visit. What are the guards, mere soldiers, doing there if Hamlet and Horatio have a quiet chat about the death of Hamlet's father? So they appear to loiter uncomfortably.

> *Horatio*   **I saw him once; a was a goodly king.**

(Now we see them on TV every day, rammed down our throats.) Eventually, after some light and polite chat, Hamlet feeds him the line –

> *Hamlet*   **I shall not look upon his like again.**

During this we have taken a slow stroll around the stage. Horatio, grabbing this for his cue, counters with –

> *Horatio*   **My lord, I think I saw him yesternight.**

A difficult one, this, to feign surprise or misunderstanding.

> *Hamlet*   **Saw? Who?**

A small break just renders the hint that something not quite gelling is slipping in.

> *Horatio*   **My lord, the King your father.**

Another bitch to look completely stunned, amazed, when you know exactly what is about to be said. To lie on stage is difficult. One can say a thousand times, *To be or not to be, that is the question*, since an abstract, philosophical or emotional statement contains an eternal truth that one will always believe in. But to create a false sense of surprise is lying because the audience knows very well that you know. But you go through the game.

So sometimes it would be (cynical), 'The King . . . my father?'

or (astounded), 'The King my father!!'

or (oh yes, tell me another), 'The . . . King. My *father*?'

I usually left the mystery on, 'Saw . . . who?' A bit Noël Coward. 'What did you say, old chap? I didn't quite catch it.' And rushed into, 'The King!! My father.'

or, 'What are you saying? Are you trying to unhinge me?' Just traces of anger lining the edges.

Horatio calls or snaps his fingers for the witnesses to make themselves felt. They come right in and stand either side of the circle. Horatio goes into his spiel. I walk around slowly, looking at them, and try to take all this in.

Hamlet   **But where was this?**

Still casual, with a flick on *was*.

   Did you not speak to it?

Feelings now beginning to come in of a son's concern. But also, being a prince, I have a slightly demanding concern as of one dealing with people whose intelligence is lower.

   'Tis very strange.

A little twist here which resulted in a response of laughter from the audience. I did not go out to gain a laugh but wanted to escape from this overall lie and mock concern. I would rather not be manipulated so easily. Like, 'You're not telling me a tall one, are you? Not drunk again?' So Horatio counters quite strongly to dispel any slur on his observation:

Horatio   **As I do live, my honour'd lord, 'tis true;**
   And we did think it writ down in our duty
   To let you know of it.

Realizing I have gone too far in my suspicion I give:

Hamlet   **Indeed, sirs; but this troubles me.**

I then decide to make a few gentle inquiries. I might be in court. Hamlet makes a great play about his tables and I assume he carries a little notebook around to make some notes to remind himself of some event, write the odd love note, etc. So now I take out this little book. Why bring it out just on *my tables* [I, v]? Such an odd time to write down his passions after the Ghost has left. So why not now? So now, as he interrogates, he puts down their answers. This taking out of the little book naturally brought a little titter from the punters, but yet again this is such a famous scene that I wanted to make it as personal to me as possible and not keep giving these false reactions. Ah yes, and it's not false to come out with your notebook and impersonate

Hercule Poirot? Perhaps, but it is so outrageous in the actual scene and yet it makes a great kind of sense to Hamlet's practical mind.

I remember when I was an assistant at seventeen years of age in a shop in Regent Street I always had a little book, and whenever the manager annoyed me I would go into a corner and scribble furiously and spew out all my hate. You write what burns in your breast, and you have no one to spew it out to and so you bury your atomic waste in the safe confines of your little book. I suppose I wanted to justify its later use, but later in the run of the production I got rid of the book when it fell out of my pocket. I found it a nuisance. Some of the cast were relieved.

Hamlet   **I would I had been there.**

Horatio   **It would have much amaz'd you.**

Hamlet   **Very like.**

Now I chuckled here with a kind of nervousness as if there were a thrilling kind of horror to be obtained – as if it might not be my father at all. All it is now is a ghost that resembles him. But it is rather . . . It would have scared the shit out of me . . . '*Veeeerry* like.'

Hamlet   **I will watch tonight.**

Perchance 'twill walk again.

Horatio   **I war'nt it will.**

I almost challenge Horatio that it won't while he confirms its appearance. Then a decision to speak to it. They go . . . swiftly . . . check the time first . . .

Hamlet   **'twixt eleven and twelve**

I'll visit you.

I am alone and muse on the information I have been given. Not just my father's spirit, but in arms. So he must have something very urgent to say if he is lugging all that armour around.

Hamlet   **Foul deeds will rise,**

Though all the earth o'erwhelm them, to men's eyes.

The smell of bad things will always lead you to its source. I feel strangely alone at this point. I can only say this speech simply and directly, and leave.

19

SCENE III

Laertes and Ophelia.

As I leave, it is a cue to change the scene, to make it ready for the next with Laertes and Ophelia. We break up the chairs, impersonating porters and the mêlée of a crowded port. The chairs are carried as if luggage. We hear shouts of, 'All aboard . . .'

Laertes runs in with a case. The chairs are now on the outer square. The actors are all sitting around the stage on different chairs and are quite still. The piano is rendering an old tune of the thirties appropriate to the mood.

I return to the folds of the chorus and watch. We are always on the stage watching the proceedings, as if the evidence at a trial was unfolding. I cannot discuss Laertes since he is not me. I am writing from my point of view and can discuss him only in so far as he affects me. Scholars have written about the whole play and each character with total objectivity, but I can see Laertes only from the outside, and I see an interfering turd who gives to all advice he cannot live by. A cheat, an opportunist. He is interfering with the very genuine love I have for Ophelia, saying,

Hold it a fashion and a toy in blood. . .

Really. Does he mean that I am only a toy whose enchantment will pass with maturity; only that I happen to be filled with blood rather than sawdust? Or is he being slightly dirty? The beast. He rhapsodizes about love in general:

> **A violet in the youth of primy nature,**
> **Forward, not permanent, sweet, not lasting,**
> **The perfume and suppliance of a minute,**
> **No more.**

So Laertes holds himself to be the arbiter of love. Also:

Perhaps he loves you now . . .

Now he is on a different tack. Now I have no will – even if my love *is* genuine, while before he was sure I was a toy in blood. Now political reasons abound. It is still a worthless relationship since I have no say in the running of my life. The state must determine my choice and I will end up marrying some decayed, buck-toothed princess from England in order to strengthen the dynasty.

> **Then weigh what loss your honour may sustain**
> **If with too credent ear you list his songs,**
> **Or lose your heart, or your chaste treasure open . . .**

Ah, *now* we are getting to the crunch. He paints some very lubricious pictures in her skull which leave little to the imagination – don't make the beast with two backs. That is what he is saying in so many words. Laertes is such a model of Danish rectitude – though he is a brothel-creeper in Paris and needs the spies sent by his father lest he whore and drink himself into dissolution. People who indulge are so willing to warn others against their own proclivities. For a crook, the world is full of crooks. Still not satisfied, Laertes sluices yet more carnal images through the sewer he carries in his brain:

> **The canker galls the infants of the spring**
> **Too oft before their buttons be disclos'd,**
> **And in the morn and liquid dew of youth**
> **Contagious blastments are most imminent.**
> **Be wary then . . .**

He finishes. Ophelia here giggles at the absurd rodomontade of his speech – his evasiveness and his absurd euphemism for what she and Hamlet have probably been having twice daily for months – and that is a good wholesome screw. The nunnery scene contains the language of a betrayed lover, not the anger or petulance of those who have not reached a profound intimacy of the body. So Laertes, not liking this giggle of hers, closes with:

> **Fear it, Ophelia . . .**
> . . .
> **best safety lies in fear.**

What Calvinistic advice – a harsh, Christian concept of freedom. Fear. Not understanding – decency even – but fear. Fear only the Laerteses of this world: clean, upright, noble-seeming and repressive bastards. Ophelia joshes him and punctures his own inflated ideas with her last speech, and, on the last line, ruffles his hair – which he is quick to repair.

21

Barry Philips as Laertes advising his sister. A very gentle scene, beautifully played, with Chloë Salaman as our second Ophelia.

Ophelia has been wearing her severe, two-piece suit with white blouse and high-heeled shoes. She looks very sedate and yet has a languorous quality. Sally Bentley was a classical dancer and had a way of making very definite statements about her body on stage. She is nothing like an actress and played Ophelia with rare delicacy and politeness. She is not the type of actress we are accustomed to seeing later in the mad scene, lifting her dress up and walking round with her head tilted on one side in the traditional modern manner. Her madness is already there. In her sweetness and excessive gentleness there is already a withdrawal from the world. She is the third Ophelia I have worked with, and while the others had excellent qualities, they were still actresses, whereas Sally *was* Ophelia.

On comes fat Polonius, sweating under his greatcoat, with his short, Prussian, parted haircut and his little Hitler moustache. He looked like a butler, or the Kitchener First World War poster, YOUR COUNTRY NEEDS YOU! He is a perfect Polonius. We are bored to death by the old farts usually dug up to go over one of the most

22

famous scenes: old fart lets out his bag of advice while Laertes and Ophelia play mischievously behind him. Then old fart turns round and they giggle innocently while the audience from Surrey smiles benevolently at having understood this – the boringest scene in Christendom. We do not intend to bore the audience since we are not in that kind of business.

So Polonius enters, having walked all the way upstage and turned left, walked to centre and entered the room. There are ten commandments to observe in these few precepts. Each one is a worthy comment on values and maybe one to seize on in times of difficulties or indecision. But they are also the careful rules of the bourgeoisie; the prudent rules of bourgeois Teutonic husbandry: don't lend so you don't borrow. Just in case your friend can't pay you back . . .

Polonius **Give every man thy ear, but few thy voice** . . .
– don't risk retort or abuse –
      Costly thy habit . . .
Yes; like a smart businessman, silently signalling wealth but without freedom or spirit – no elaboration. But on the whole these are sensible homilies for a man in Laertes's position.

Laertes and Ophelia perform a mimetic demonstration of the speech as if they were illustrating a lecture. It is very deliberate and performed in a *commedia dell'arte* style in counterpoint to what Polonius is saying. While they are illustrating, they are not really duplicating what Polonius is saying so much as satirizing it and performing like those old fairground 'passions'. They do it expertly and sometimes it looks like a mannequin show. The exercise serves to refresh the audience and make the familiar unfamiliar and new.

The drum rolls and the actors get into their positions ready to start. Then Polonius begins. The mime is funny and satirically exaggerates the truisms so that the truth rebounds with more force – in the way a cartoon might capture salient features. Also it places the actors out of the heroic mould of 'I am playing Laertes or Ophelia' and back into the roles of two players having fun. The scene works well and this is the sole justification for it. It is a scene – if you like – that is already in

23

italics and so to make it more so seems not only appropriate but necessary. However

This above all: to thine own self be true . . .

requires nothing and we did nothing except stop and listen. Polonius hugs Laertes and Laertes Ophelia. Polonius hands Laertes the case he was in danger of forgetting and Laertes leaves. As he does so the cast becomes the family waving farewell. Eventually they all sit, this time facing in one direction. Laertes goes and rejoins the sea of faces from whence he came. He is now a player. Polonius and Ophelia stand there waving to a figure whose diminishing, receding shape matches their gradually declining waves.

A NOTE ABOUT PLAYING IN THE ROUND: THE OBVIOUS BENEFITS OF PLAYING IN THE ROUND ARE ENORMOUS, IF YOU CAN USE THEM. ONE IS EXPOSED ON ALL SIDES AND IT IS A DIFFERENT PICTURE FOR ALL . . . A TURN OF THE HEAD OR BODY AND THE WHOLE BEING IS USED. YOU DON'T GET BAKED ON ONE SIDE ONLY AND SO YOU START TO FEEL YOURSELF IN A THREE-DIMENSIONAL STATE. THEREFORE THE SQUARE DOES RESEMBLE A BOXING RING. NO PART OF THE BODY IS LESS INTERESTING THAN ANOTHER PART. A BACK HAS GREAT POWER AND SOMETIMES SUGGESTS FAR MORE BY OMISSION. OUR EXAMINATION OF THE PLAY TAKES ON A LECTURE-PLUS-DEMONSTRATION QUALITY IN THE ROUND AS THE AUDIENCE PEERS DOWN ON US. AND YOU NEED HAVE NO MEMBER OF THE AUDIENCE MORE THAN THREE OR FOUR ROWS AWAY. THE EXPERIENCE CAN BECOME INTENSE FOR THEM AS WELL AS FOR US: THEY CAN WATCH THEMSELVES IN THE FACES OF THE SPECTATORS OPPOSITE, THE FOUR SIDES SOMEHOW LINKING ENERGIES WITH US, LOCKED IN THE MIDDLE WITH NO ESCAPE. A SQUARE OF FLESH. THE LIGHT ON THE WHOLE TIME. ONE BRIGHT, WHITE LIGHT. EVERYONE SEEN. NO CHANCE FOR ESCAPE. THE RITUAL HAS ITS RULES THAT MAKE YOU AN ALIEN DURING THE PERIOD OF PERFORMANCE. YOU ARE THE SACRIFICE AND YOU DISSECT YOUR-SELF WITH THE SCALPEL CALLED HAMLET AND PEEL OFF THE FLESH AND NERVES IN FRONT OF THE AUDIENCE. THEY ARE CLOSE

AND YOU CANNOT CHEAT WITH PULLING FACES UPSTAGE – AS WE DID WHEN WE WERE PUT INTO A PROSCENIUM-ARCH THEATRE – OR SNEAK A BREATHER, OR REFLECT ON THE SHORTCOMINGS OF A SPEECH. YOU ARE ROASTED IN THE ROUND. YOU MUST POUR YOURSELF INTO THIS CREATURE HAMLET OR POUR HIM INTO YOU. YOU SEE YOUR FRIENDS IN THE FRONT AS YOU SIT FOR THE FIRST SCENE. O GOD, I WISH I HADN'T SEEN THEM BUT INCREASE CONCENTRATION AND OVERCOME. STOP BEING AWARE OF ANYONE. THE INTENSITY INCREASES YOUR PERFORMANCE POWER SINCE YOU HAVE REVVED UP TO OVERCOME THEIR PRESENCE. NOW YOU DON'T KNOW THEM ANY MORE. THEY HAVE FADED INTO THE SEA OF SPECTATORS AND THEIR PRESENCE MERELY FUELS YOU. YOU DON'T KNOW ANYONE EXCEPT WHO YOU AND THE OTHER CHARACTERS ARE. YOU ARE PREPARED TO CARESS, HOWL, SCREAM, CRY WITH OR AT PEOPLE WITH WHOM YOU WILL AFTERWARDS FEEL AWKWARD OR EVEN SHY. ZEN IN THE ART OF HAMLET. TO BE. TO BECOME ONE WITH THE FLOW. HAMLET IS THE TEACHER TEACHING HIS PHILOSOPHY AT EVERY TURN. A SCENE IS PLAYED ALMOST AS A DEMONSTRATION FOR HAMLET TO ANALYSE FOR US. AS IF HE SETS IT UP . . . *Is it not monstrous that this player here* . . . *Witness this army of such mass and charge* . . . *To be or not to be* . . . *So, oft it chances in particular men* . . . HE IS ALWAYS INTERPRETING AND REFLECTING ON LIFE IN THE PAST OR THAT WHICH HAS JUST GONE. HE IS THE MASTER THROUGH SHAKESPEARE. BUT THE TEST IS IN OVERCOMING HIS OWN FLAWS.

Ophelia and Polonius.

The actors have waved goodbye. This was also a ruse to let them melt and become the walls of the castle or just figures who wait for their cues; sometimes like retainers, or servants, or people waiting. A fresco: some listeners, eavesdroppers, spies. Polonius has started to question Ophelia in a polite, fatherly way; yet he too is contaminated by this lust thing – just like Laertes. Again, affection has become perilous –

Polonius   **springes to catch woodcocks.**

He is angry – at least in the way David Auker plays it, he is blood-boiled with fury. We have seen him now walk down the corridors followed by Ophelia who trails wistfully after him. He continues his walk round the stage and then across, each time defining the structure that we are in. We create chambers and antechambers. Ophelia, with her innocent intentions, pleads her case, but is countered with the model of repressed passion of a very English type:

> **I do know,**
> **When the blood burns, how prodigal the soul**
> **Lends the tongue vows. These blazes, daughter,**
> **Giving more light than heat . . .**
>
> **. . .**
>
> **You must not take for fire.**

Of course he knows. He has probably made these vows in heat himself, for goods he could not then pay for. He is another who sees the world in his own image: as corrupt, cheating, lying, spying and stupid. He brought up his children so well that he indirectly causes both their deaths, and his own. As a result of his apparently rigid adherence to principle his son has become corrupt in revolt, and his daughter a mealy-mouthed wet, bullied into subservience by two sexually repressed, dirt-seeking men. Polonius claims he knows when the blood burns! How? The fact is that I do love Ophelia and it must be difficult for her to hold on to her sanity with those two right-wing bastards basting her mind with their warnings of *buttons, chastity, maids, chaste treasure, springes, perilous, beguile, blood, blazes,* etc., etc. They are trying to protect her virginity like some holy relic to be kept under lock and key.

During this scene we must imagine that we are transported to the corridors of the castle. People are walking up and down the corridors. Polonius is now walking up and down the corridor followed by a tearful and pleading Ophelia. They stop, and he offers some judgement, and on they go again with Polonius tearing down the passages. Now two people meet and chat, and Ophelia and Polonius pass them, nodding and lowering their voices until they are out of earshot. The cast makes up these distractions to suggest the activity of the castle and the constantly alert and travelling ear. Meanwhile, two others have met and become a double door for Polonius and Ophelia to pass through, and then immediately become passers-by when they have served their function as doors.

So we witness a functioning castle served by stewards and all sorts of characters who might be employed in various occupations. The text is broken and filtered through this activity and the distraction seems to compel the audience to listen and watch the scene. In most productions the scene is static, and a restless mind will therefore find distractions. Any odd noise or disturbance will be seized on gratefully by a mind that is being starved of information.

In the earlier scene the ten commandments of Polonius somehow make the assumption that the rest of the world is without them. He has the full monopoly of wisdom, manners and, now, sexual behaviour, and so stamps on any possibility of fruition between Hamlet and Ophelia. Of course the plot demands this at the same time, and many directors will spend endless hours boring the cast to death with lengthy expositions regarding characters, when they are totally unreal and many contradict themselves continually for the sake of the plot. Still, many directors don't feel they have done their job unless they have impressed the cast with their knowledge of the play or their opinion on it – even if the subsequent production is as boring as old socks, which it invariably is.

HOWEVER, IN THIS CASE HAMLET IS A DANGER TO POLONIUS'S PRESENT EMPLOYER. HAMLET SPOKE HIS MIND IN THE ASSEMBLY OR COURT, MAKING A SPLENDID COMMENTARY ON APPEARANCES WHICH WAS BOTH INSULTING AND BRAVELY FORWARD. CLAUDIUS'S REGARD FOR THE DEAD KING WAS AS FULSOMELY HYPOCRITICAL AS – SAY – THE GOVERNMENT'S CROCODILE TEARS OVER THE BRITISH DEATHS CAUSED IN THE FALKLANDS WAR. ACTS OF POLITICAL OR MILITARY MURDER ARE FUELLED OFTEN BY THE SAME MOTIVATIONS. IT IS NO SECRET THAT ORDERS WERE GIVEN

TO FIRE ON THE SHIP, THE *BELGRANO*, WHEN IT WAS WAY OUTSIDE THE 200-MILE-RADIUS EXCLUSION ZONE. SO I SUPPOSE KING HAMLET'S DEATH WAS NOT MOTIVATED BY ANYTHING MUCH HIGHER OR LOWER: A DESIRE FOR POWER. WE WERE TOURING EUROPE WITH *HAMLET* WHEN THE FALKLANDS WAR WAS IN FULL SWING AND, TO AN ACTOR, THE WHOLE COMPANY FELT THE MOST EXTREME REVULSION FOR THIS HORRIBLE WASTE OF HUMAN LIFE. THE PERFORMANCE OF THIS PLAY EACH NIGHT, AND EVEN THE PROXIMITY OF TWELVE YOUNG PEOPLE AND THEIR HOPES AND IDEALS, PLUS THE PLAYING, MAY HAVE MADE US EVEN MORE INTOLERANT THAN USUAL. WE FOUND CONTINUOUS REINFORCE- MENT IN SHAKESPEARE'S WORDS FOR THE PETTY AND UNIMAGI- NATIVE ACTS OF MAN — OR, RATHER, OF POLITICIANS. IN CONSEQUENCE CERTAIN SCENES SEEMED UNDERLINED FOR US. SO HAMLET IS NOT COMPLYING WITH THE DUNG-HEAP MORALITY THAT PASSES FOR GOVERNMENT, ANY MORE THAN A HAMLET TODAY COULD. HAMLET HAS LEARNED SOMETHING IN WITTEN- BERG APART FROM PHILOSOPHY, AND THAT KNOWLEDGE WILL BE THE DOWNFALL OF HIMSELF AND ALL AROUND HIM. IN THE END, POLONIUS'S CONCERN FOR OPHELIA IS MORE CONCERN FOR POLONIUS, AND SO IN EFFECT HIS WARNING IS A POLITICAL ACT.

> *Polonius* **Come your ways.**
> *Ophelia* **I shall obey, my lord.**

David Auker, the Fatty Arbuckle of the group and, in my opinion, the best Polonius I've seen, was a frightening bully to Ophelia and would jab her cruelly with his bowler as he left. He had a streak of sadism which could not cope with the soppy or soft and would almost have too much energy for his rage to siphon off, and so was a steaming cauldron when he was not being an unctuous toe-licker with the King and Queen. He reminded me of one of those head waiters in the large hotels, bullying the skivvies and greasing the customers.

As they sit, joining the line, up the wind starts and we are on the battlements once more.

SCENE IV

The three of us walk to centre as Polonius and Ophelia return to their places. My collar is up and so is Horatio's. We walk up and down the line in the centre of the stage. The seated actors create a cold whining wind.

Hamlet   **What hour now?**
Horatio   **I think it lacks of twelve.**

It's getting near the time. A shred of fear plucks courage from us when we hear the sound of laughter and boisterous drunken revelry. The line becomes a grotesque group of gargoyles, leering and lurching; and we are able to see the King at his celebration –

Hamlet   **The King doth wake tonight and takes his rouse,**
                 Keeps wassail, and the swagg'ring upspring reels. . .

Their sound stops to enable us to talk but the action goes on in silence, which renders them almost more horrific.

I talk about inherited customs, and really Shakespeare could be talking about the British way of life today, in a place he conveniently names Denmark. We see other nations calling us drunkards. Shakespeare was obviously a traveller. He has witnessed or at least heard of the civilized habits of other countries. He has naturally had communication with foreign visitors and been aware of the reaction they must have had to the English way of life. Europe was the cauldron of great culture which culminated in the Renaissance. An aware man like Shakespeare would naturally compare the profundity of European art and manners with those of the primitive society in which he lived.

IT IS VERY TEMPTING TO MAKE COMPARISONS WITH CONTEMPORARY SOCIETY AND FIND THAT THINGS HAVE CHANGED VERY LITTLE: THAT WE ARE STILL IN MANY WAYS THE PIGS OF EUROPE IN THE WAY THAT WE CELEBRATE OUR VICES. WE HAVE ONLY TO SEE THE RAUCOUS FESTIVITIES AND THE DRUNKEN LINE OF YOBS THAT FOLLOWS THE FOOTBALL MATCHES TO EUROPE, THE FIGHTS AND RIOTS, THE WRECKAGE THAT FOLLOWS IN THE WAKE OF ANY

MAJOR SPORTING EVENT IN EUROPE SO THAT FOREIGN STADIUMS EVEN CORDON OFF THE ENGLISH OR SCOTS FOOTBALL FANS AS IF THEY WERE MAD BEASTS! THE BRITISH RELEASE THEIR FRUST-RATION THROUGH BOOZE, WHICH HAS BEEN THE TRADITIONAL METHOD TO DULL AN OPPRESSIVE CLASS-RIDDEN SOCIETY, AN UNDERPAID MASS OF WORKERS WHO WOULD FIND NO JOY OTHER THAN THE GROTTY PUB. SUCCESSIVE POLITICAL AND MONARCHIS-TIC REGIMES HAVE TREATED THE WORKER IN THIS COUNTRY AS ALWAYS SOMETHING SLIGHTLY LESS THAN DIRT, AND POVERTY WAS ENDEMIC TO ANYONE WITH LITTLE EDUCATION. THE STANDARD OF LIVING — EVEN IN THE EARLY PART OF THIS CENTURY WHEN THE NATION WAS ONE OF THE WORLD'S RICHEST — WAS THE LOWEST IN THE WESTERN WORLD. REFER TO JACK LONDON'S *THE ABYSS*, IN WHICH HE DESCRIBES STANDARDS AMONG THE POOR AS LOW AS, IF NOT LOWER THAN, THE ESKI-MOS'. CHEAP DRINK SEEMED TO BE THE ONLY PANACEA AND ESCAPE ROUTE. THERE WAS NO OTHER WAY OF ESCAPE — WHEN YOU COULD, YOU EMIGRATED. FAILING THAT, YOU TOOK TO DRINK.

ONE NIGHT I WAS PLAYING HAMLET AT THE ROUND HOUSE WHEN THE BAR DECIDED TO SHUT EARLY AS THERE WEREN'T ENOUGH PEOPLE WHO WANTED A DRINK AT THE END OF A PERFORMANCE. SO WE MADE A MAD DASH ACROSS THE ROAD TO AN EVIL-SMELLING PUB IN CAMDEN TOWN. AFTER THREE HOURS OF PLAYING WE HAD OUR TONGUES HANGING OUT. THEN WE WERE PLACED IN THE POSITION OF HAVING TO BEG SOME SURLY BARMAN TO ALLOW US A DRINK IF THE CLOCK SHOWED A FEW SECONDS PAST TIME. THE POWERS VESTED IN THE BARMAN BY THESE RIDICU-LOUSLY STUPID AND CLASS-MADE LAWS TURNED THE BARMAN INTO A SADIST WHO WOULD DISPENSE RELIEF ACCORDING TO HIS WHIM.

ONE NIGHT I SAW DUSTIN HOFFMAN IN THE AUDIENCE. HE CAME BACKSTAGE FULL OF THE KIND OF REAL ENTHUSIASM THAT HE HAD NOT BEEN ABLE TO DISPLAY AT ANY OF THE OTHER PRODUCTIONS HE HAD SEEN IN LONDON — WHICH INCLUDED A

RIVAL *HAMLET*. HOWEVER, WE ALL GATHERED ON THE PAVEMENT
WITH NE'ER A PLACE TO GO. SO, THERE WE WERE ON A WIND-
SWEPT CORNER OF THIS CIVILIZATION: ONE OF AMERICA'S FINEST
ACTORS AND ME AND THE CAST ON THE STREET, HOLDING A
CONVERSATION THAT, BY THE NATURE OF THE ENVIRONMENT,
HAD TO BE BRIEF.

Hamlet   . . . **though perform'd at height** . . .
We Brits have been known for our achievements though these are
mitigated or somewhat sullied by the drink problem. But the speech
is about nationhood as well as the collective personality. To have a
flaw colours everything that you do. So Hamlet would be seeking too
much perfection. He has no time for the flaws that we, with our
British amateurism, regard as 'only human'. For Hamlet the flaw is
not a colouring or a character quirk; it is a corruption of vital energy
and he seeks perfection as the natural attainment mankind should
seek. Hamlet is outgoing, purposeful, and has an aim or goal which is
his very watchfulness. He is a moral warrior who must not be tainted
by decadence. He will avenge a death; he will weigh up the pros and
cons and examine every particle of evidence for any flaw that might
result in a miscarriage of justice. He must be certain. Hamlet must be
without flaw as, from his lofty perch, he hears the rabble of the world:

> **This heavy-headed revel east and west**
> **Makes us traduc'd and tax'd of other nations –**
> **They clepe us drunkards, and with swinish phrase**
> **Soil our addition** . . .

It hurts his ear and his mind, for Hamlet is perfect – because he is
superhuman. He is an amalgam of all the virtues that Shakespeare
himself wishes to project on to him: the great poet living in a barbaric
society and wishing to heighten the consciousness of his audience.
But the purpose of fiction is to create the idealized self so that he may
point the way to lesser mortals.

Horatio   **Look, my lord, it comes!**
I have been looking the other way but now I hear the sounds of the

chorus and see my father making his slow walk across the stage; not as a behemoth or sepulchral being or – God forbid – a pasty creature holding a concealed torch up to his face. Our Ghost is a human person walking slowly and deliberately and *stately by them*. Now Shakespeare usually had a reason to guide us in our reading of the text. So to follow his direction doesn't seem a bad idea. I turn to face him. To see him coming slowly wrenches from me all my breath. One needs something here. A scream, but not a great howl; a silent or almost silent scream from the gut. I suck all the air into me, which impacts into my stomach and lets out a long, high-pitched whine, the piercing sound of shock waves going through me, and air is ripping at the vocal cords which are being sucked inwards. It is an eerie sound and almost the reversal of a scream. I hold my head, my lips stretched taut across my mouth. The sound fades away into the night in a long thin thread; and dissolves. I recover and say simply,

    Hamlet   **Angels and ministers of grace defend us!**
He won't simply accept this visitation as his father:

       Be thou a spirit of health or goblin damn'd . . .
Since the Ghost is wearing the outer shape of his father he will speak to it. It would have been simpler merely to shout, 'Father', but Shakespeare wants the prelude as a parenthesis to Hamlet saying,

             I'll call thee Hamlet,

      King . . .
(Still no answer.)
Now . . .

        father . . .
shouted as if he could no longer just enumerate his titles and the floodgates are lowered for this cry from the son. And then finishing with . . .

        royal Dane.
It is not that Hamlet is asking if his father is all these things, or a goblin with wicked intents; he is saying no matter what shape you visit me in, 'I'll call thee father.' In fact the preamble is to give emphasis to Hamlet's conviction in his father. Then I reasonably ask him why he is doing this:

32

> **Why thy canoniz'd bones, hearsed in death,**
> **Have burst their cerements . . . ?**

Here I must ask him why and in a confidential way – not fall into the trap of the rhetoric and poetic imagery that may swell the tongue and the heart into rolling these words around a few choice sounds; but simple – as if to a child or someone in distress – low . . . pleading . . .

> **What should we do?**

Almost helpless.

The Ghost is slowly walking all this time since he is forced to walk the night and cannot be still. So I will be Shakespeare and have the Ghost making his perambulation around the stage, beckoning me to follow – I like to follow text directions even when it is difficult for the simple reason that the lines then justify the action. (This is unlike what happened in a recent production in which the actor cleverly, and in an exorcist way, was possessed by the Ghost. This was thrilling to watch but made nonsense of the text – of a stately Ghost making his solemn march. It was a travesty of the Ghost and, though the actor was skilled, it showed yet again a director's total lack of imagination in dealing with a tricky subject. The actor pulled off the stunt and thus saved the show for the director, although the rest of the production was conventional and pedestrian and was another example of a director getting together with an actor and casting mouthpieces around him to deliver the text. So our Ghost makes his slow and stately way. I have to add these interjections and comments since I am Hamlet and must show the way the play must go – and that is towards the design of the writer. Thanks.)

I am caught in the mesmeric spell of the ghostly journey, becoming the pivotal centre as he seems to circle me as I am frozen still within. My colleagues forbid me to follow as Horatio says,

> *Horatio* **What if it tempt you toward the flood, my lord,**
> **Or to the dreadful summit of the cliff**
> **That beetles o'er his base into the sea,**
> **And there assume some other horrible form**
> **Which might deprive your sovereignty of reason**
> **And draw you into madness? Think of it.**

Horatio is cautious to the end.

    Hamlet   **Hold off your hands.**

Thus their reason and Hamlet's instinct are at war – the rational versus the poetic – reason always ready to doubt and fear the inexplicable, though Horatio has already confirmed his total belief that it is Hamlet's father:

    Horatio   **These hands are not more like.** [I, ii]

So he seems to know the old King well. And yet he also says,

    I saw him once; a was a goodly king. [I, ii]

So either Horatio knows him as well as his own hands, or he knows him slightly, as one who once in his lifetime came to the court. So one sees the discrepancies in Shakespeare and the desire to impart information and plot at the cost of a character's coherence. Thus it is difficult in a fiction to analyse characters as real flesh and blood. There is evidence in the characters' speeches but, since they are invented, one cannot give too much credence to a director who discusses fictional characters as if they were real, rather than indications of types. And the speeches are there more often than not to put opposing views to highlight the struggle of the protagonist and to create conflict. Thus someone will say – and must say –

    You shall not go . . .

just so that someone else can be heroic and say,

    Unhand me . . .

    By heaven, I'll make a ghost of him that lets me.

There is no reason in the world for the two men not to say, 'Go, but be careful', but there is no drama in that. The play is there for the drama and not necessarily for the truth. Perhaps Shakespeare's weakness is in making everyone else appear less graceful – timid, conventional – in order to make the point about the nobility of Hamlet; and the absurdity is that it creates dull characters who mouth such arrogant nonsense as *E'en so, my lord* every now and again. Probably what I am saying is that Shakespeare's characters can tend to be cardboard cut-outs designed to make Hamlet look good. They are not rounded by idiosyncratic behaviour or personal mannerisms except in a few circumstances. So, bearing this in mind, we must read that Horatio puts nefarious deeds into the will of the walking dead, so Hamlet can *bravely* oppose him.

At this stage Horatio is seizing my right hand and I am pulled while the Ghost is walking to the left of me. I pull and Marcellus takes Horatio's hand; thus our energies are pulled across the stage in a chain of flesh or a tug of war . . . Then I am leaning so far over to the left – using my right foot against his left, which secures me from

The tug of war as mates try to prevent me from going over the edge. (Note pen in top pocket!)

sliding – so that we are sculpted in our struggle into a seething mass . . . and then I hurl out the lines as if torn from me and howl to the gods . . .

> *Hamlet*   **My fate cries out**
> **And makes each petty artire in this body**
> **As hardy as the Nemean lion's nerve.**

Starting with *My*, I rather let it out as 'miiiiiiiiy', so that I can stay on a high register and sing it out on one breath . . . it is a very dramatic moment. My strength becomes super- or paranormal, and I break from the chain on:

> **By heaven, I'll make a ghost of him that lets me.**
> **I say away. – Go on, I'll follow thee.**

swinging them around in a circle and breaking them off, as if hurled by a high-powered roundabout. They are flung to the far reaches of the stage. This is grand and majestic . . . the lion's spirit roared out in hyperbole.

I stole the effect, though not the move, from Christopher Plummer with whom I had the privilege of working when we did a *Hamlet* for the BBC which was filmed at Elsinore in 1963. He has a remarkable voice with an astonishing power and I believed that he had few rivals on any stage. His Hamlet was very exciting and he had marvellous moments of inventive genius that I have never seen matched except, of course, by Olivier. Plummer had created his Hamlet with Tyrone Guthrie, who had previously created it with Olivier, so there was a good pedigree of development in the role. He had a profile and a quality of Henry Irving and was never less than inspiring. When he started *My fate cries out* he pitched almost on top C and held it there. It was one of those moments I shall never forget – and it was tempting to try to reproduce it for I could see no other way of doing it, and, whether I did it or not, I still had a go.

At the time I was in the players' scene in the production giving Lucianus, 'nephew to the king', and Lindsay Kemp was giving the Player Queen. We did it as a very stylized mime which Kemp and I worked out in great detail. I met Lindsay Kemp through our mutual interest in mime, and when I heard that Phillip Saville was directing *Hamlet* for the BBC I promptly offered myself for a part in the production. I was told that the only parts left were for players who were good mimes. I hastened to offer all my credentials as a mime – studied with Jacques Le Coq in Paris, etc., and was given a role and was able to involve Lindsay. I believe our contribution was much appreciated. Now it seems a long way away, with most of the characters or players real ghosts: the late Robert Shaw as Claudius, and the late Alec Clunes as Polonius, the late Roy Kinnear as the Gravedigger and the unknown Donald Sutherland as Fortinbras, while Michael Caine gave his Horatio – not unlike our Gary Whelan – so it was a formidable line-up. We shot it at Elsinore through storm and tempest and it was an exciting introduction to Shakespeare.

I remember Alec Clunes, who was something of a Shakespeare scholar, trying to inform Saville about the niceties of the text and generally trying to be gently instructive to a director who, although raw in Shakespeare, was a master in the field of television. One day, during a formal line-up in court, Clunes suggested that in the role of Polonius and closest to the court, he should be first in the line-up. Saville replied that sometimes 'authenticity can be the enemy of creativity', since the shot was more interesting the way he had constructed it. That remark was kept in my closet for future use. I also remember the final run-through, when the producer and all the technical staff came to watch. No one was allowed in or out – even to go to the loo. Plummer let rip a performance which I shall never forget, and at the end there was the kind of silence that made any speech afterwards seem totally ridiculous. Nobody could speak. We were, in the famous cliché, speechless. So Robert Shaw broke the ice. Our dear late Robert Shaw was very competitive.

Anyway, there are moments when a great actor serves the cause of the theatre with his own aura and makes theatre electric, and even transcends the role so that the role serves him and he becomes the genius served by the text which is subjugated by his will, and that is the only theatre I believe in. It is naturally a marrying of both, but the sum total of human inspiration relies ultimately on the actor. It is when you are at one with your own being and the role, and the forces of instinct and reason marry up and go on to the same path. At such times you can do no wrong. The ground opens up and the air seems to be cut before you. You are centred inside yourself and the words have taken you right there. You are clear, purged, summoned and possessed, but only possessed to serve something greater than yourself. The text opens the door and out comes the tiger. You seem released in displays of passion that you never exhibit in your life: as if the very passions that have been suppressed by civilized behaviour are discharged to the same extent that they have been withheld.

There is an element of unpredictability or danger in releasing the caged tiger. It is there, waiting to leap out. It has been fed not with meat but with frustration. It is an unknown quantity. It is the beast one fears. At the same time it is the danger that lies within. So I expect that what people mean when they say an actor has danger is that he does what is unexpected; or, in other words, he is not programmed by the simple responses and conditioning that makes us familiar with what he will do . . . the same Shakespearian readings we see in TV Shakespeare, the same dropping of the end of lines and the same dreary inflexion, and we know that this person's tiger will never be released. The tiger somehow takes us in leaps and bounds to the unexpected since he is releasing the passion that is revolutionary. It comes from deep within, from an area of consciousness that is primitive and instinctive. Olivier is one of those actors. It is releasing also the joy of being alive – in Spain it is called *duende*. The moment of truth when you can do no wrong. The barnstorming drunk will not possess it; neither will your extrovert actors, since they already release so much energy in their lives. It will be closer to the spirit of the introvert or neurotic: whose fires have been carefully stoked and banked and not let out wastefully. It comes from a system that has had to suppress its feelings and therefore works things out internally. Consequently it is a nervous system that is finely tuned to register the slightest tremor; in other words, uncoarse. A fine seismograph to register vibrations in the atmosphere. I once read of Paul Scofield that his voice, and therefore his mind, was like a compass that sought out every possible permutation before the needle came to rest. If our telescopes can register the light of dead stars, so can our great actors register the original thoughts of dead masters.

Hamlet throws them off and follows the Ghost. Marcellus throws out the famous line:

Something is rotten in the state of Denmark.

I wonder if Shakespeare is using Denmark as a cover for his comments on England, just as Hamlet puts an antic disposition on: again, a camouflage.

The chorus sits in a line with utmost concentration. The Ghost moves as if on strings, as if he is being pulled slowly and deliberately along the stage. I follow him slowly, just keeping pace behind his gaunt, six-foot-three-inch back. Wolf Kahler completely enters into the scene . . . his concentration is immense and intense. I know that he is totally in and feeling the part with every ounce of his being. This German, who would never get a chance to play here because he has an accent, is for me one of the most interesting actors I have ever worked with. This sounds like a list of eulogies but it is true to say that I found a bunch of warriors, since I was not looking for the kind of twits who can normally be found thrusting their piping voices in our traditional Shakespearian evenings. The actors worked with every part of their being, using every muscle and every possibility open to their imagination. They were encouraged to be brave and open and courageous. We tried to bring Shakespeare to life. So Wolf Kahler with his lantern-jutting jaw trod his stately way with the grip of a man who knows what he is doing, while the chorus was making this unearthly sound which is just the undertow. Then his voice, breaking over rocks and coming from depths too terrible to imagine. We decided to experiment with the old cliché of deep, dark, sepulchral voice for the Ghost. It worked, and shook everybody, since no human voice could sound like this. It was by pushing the voice deep into the chest and sounding as if it was coming up from a bed of concrete. It worked, and at the same time could be very moving.

> *Ghost* **Mark me.**
>
> *Hamlet* **I will.**

So simple at last. Just: *I will*. At last Shakespeare forsakes rhetoric and is simple and clear. I follow and listen, eyes wide. He continues circling the stage as if I am walking for miles around the parapets of a huge castle. But on the stage the circle is getting smaller and smaller as he seems to be tying me up in a web with me imprisoned in the centre.

The Ghost delivers his tale of horror that can leave no doubt as to the decision to be taken. Taken in his sleep . . . everlasting fire . . .

> *Ghost* **foul crimes done in my days of nature**
> **Are burnt and purg'd away.**

What crimes? I thought he was a paragon of virtue but in those days I don't doubt that guilt was the daily bread and it was not difficult to imagine yourself to be as full of guilt as you are of virtue; or to imagine

Wolf Kahler leads me into the icy regions, and I forgot my gloves!

yourself guilty all the time since Christian guilt over the sheer joy of being alive must have tormented many. But what crimes? We are to see that he is *the front of Jove himself*. A perfect being . . .

> **Hamlet** **A station like the herald Mercury**
>   **New-lighted on a heaven-kissing hill** . . . [III, iv]

This doesn't refer only to his looks since we must infer great qualities in the likes of Jove and Mercury. But again this is merely a contrast to show the inferiority of Claudius. No matter it flies in the face of truth; or even the text, or breaks down *the pales and forts of reason* [I, iv]. It seems that Claudius killed the King and that he has to pay for somebody else's crimes. But he can't mean that he is being punished for the crime of having himself murdered. Yet that is what it implies: that, since he was taken full of bread and unable to purge himself of his great sins, he is now in a place that sounds to me suspiciously like hell.

Revenge is now the keynote and Hamlet is being wound up by the most ghastly description of murder combined with sexual guilt that could fall on any ear: revenge and revenge on everything.

> *Ghost* **'Tis given out that, sleeping in my orchard,**
> **A serpent stung me . . .**

A neat image of Claudius – but a serpent in the cold climes of Denmark? Still, a serpent is a good Freudian image for sex, poison, evil, and snake-like Claudius. King Hamlet was dispatched by noxious poison in his ear – again, a good image or metaphor for the whole state that is being poisoned by a lie. A strange way to kill someone, and medically impossible, but the metaphor is too good not to use since it connects the *whole ear* being poisoned with the King's. One wonders if the idea of the poison in the ear came after Shakespeare wrote:

> *Ghost*   **so the whole ear of Denmark**
> **Is by a forged process of my death**
> **Rankly abus'd.**

There is much talk of corruption from that particular fault: *corruption, poison, incest, lust, deception, lascivious beast* . . . These words seem to stud the crown of the play like evil jewels or a glistening serpent – all words with masses of *s*'s again.

No need to itemize the sexual repression that is expressed in the play in the Ghost's speech and, before, in Hamlet's. It would seem that the old King was upset by his wife's infidelity to what after all is now his corpse. Not only the marrying which was hasty for the protection of the state but for the actual greasy bed that she would be sharing with Claudius. This is most horrible –

> *Ghost* **O, horrible! O, horrible! most horrible!**

So the son must take on the burden of the crime and engage in retribution since he must avenge not only the murder but the lust as well.

> *Ghost* **Let not the royal bed of Denmark be**
> **A couch for luxury and damned incest.**

In other words I must take on the guilt. The horrible image in the mind's eye of the murderer bedding my mother. Horrible indeed. So the canker is in the bed as well as the state. Dirty Hamlet . . . dirty

Ophelia . . . dirty Claudius. Buttons and mildew, lust and garbage. And masses of hissing prick-like snakes. Touches of Strindberg and great woman-hatred. So the Ghost entwines Hamlet's mind in the incestuous spunk-stained sheets.

As the Ghost traverses the stage telling the story, Hamlet remains still in the centre as the Ghost winds the story round him. Hamlet covers his ears – he can barely stand the acid dropping into them. Hamlet becomes the murdered King. The story curdles Hamlet's own brain as if the Ghost were pouring and relieving some of his own poisoned cells into Hamlet. Hamlet twitches and convulses . . . howls with the Ghost. The Ghost vanishes; rather, he walks slowly away with a long-drawn-out –

Ghost   **Remember me**eeee

Hamlet intones with the Ghost's *me* a long –

> *Hamlet*   **OOOOOO all you host of heaven! O earth! What else?**
>
> **And shall I couple hell?**

– as if they are mingling their blood with their voices.

I have collapsed on the *O*. It is the only thing I can think of doing. I have been kept upright by the hatred instilled in me and now as the Ghost goes it is as if the strings in me have been cut and my legs just collapse, useless and withered beneath me. Only my voice; a long slow sound being drawn out of my bowels. I get up. It is always an awkward one for me. I feel I have to collapse, but then to get up with such a line –

> *Hamlet*   **And you, my sinews, grow not instant old,**
>
> **But bear me stiffly up.**

It is difficult to act out precisely what you are saying. Once I just lay there staring at the ceiling and it felt good just to lie there. And another time I just collapsed to my knees and then over on to my face until I was just a ball of pain, which seemed better. It must be clear and direct from now on. Quiet resolve: the intense determination to wipe the slate clean of anything that went before, anything but this.

Suddenly you have a role to play and a task, the performing of which will highlight everything in its path. When you are given a

Try to imagine a blood-curdling scream coming out of my mouth, or invent your own caption.

difficult role to do – whether as an actor or in life – the effort that is summoned up is also going to throw out much that was of value before. Suddenly the task makes men of us: we are engaging all our equipment, all our mental faculties and courage to deal with it, and in dealing with it we also find much in our pre-role life that was insipid. Or the role brightens the light we carry in our minds – the searchlight that gets dim with constant self-interest. Now it is like a fire lighting everything in its path. Beware those who are exposed to it – nothing seems right again. Everything is vapid, silly, useless and pretend; only what is vital is worth living for and the meaning of life and the values for which you lay down your life suddenly become very clear. I

43

suppose that this is what happens to Hamlet. Or Joseph K in Kafka's *The Trial*. He is on trial for a crime he did not commit or have any knowledge of. But in searching for the source of his offence he grows into the man he may not have been before. The task winds us up. It screws our courage to the sticking place. Always in Shakespeare there is a task to perform that will make or break us. In the end it reveals us. I am getting closer to the heart of Shakespeare and this analysis is making him reveal himself to me under the guise of Hamlet . . . just as England is under the guise of Denmark, just as I am revealed to myself under the guise of Hamlet. All acting is a quest for self anyway. So now it is quiet determination until the flash of his mother flies into his mind . . .

O most pernicious woman!

I could kill him now. Now I could go straight there to where even at this moment they are making the two-backed beast. But no . . . no . . . the first no of many . . . I'll write it down instead . . . write down,

That one may smile, and smile, and be a villain –

I take out a notebook at this critical time and start writing:

Meet it is I set it down . . .

Few actors take out a little book, but Hamlet should – he is always jotting down little notes here and there. He is an observer. Also it siphons off the rage and prevents him acting too hastily.

REMEMBER WHEN I SAID I WAS A YOUNG MAN OF SEVENTEEN AND WORKING IN A GENTS' OUTFITTERS IN REGENT STREET? THE MANAGER ALWAYS WANTED TO INGRATIATE HIMSELF WITH THE LADIES. SO, WHENEVER A PRETTY GIRL CAME IN, HE WOULD STRETCH HIS OAFISH UGLY FACE ACROSS THE COUNTER AND I WOULD EXPLODE INSIDE AND PACE TO THE END OF THE COUNTER AND TAKE OUT A LITTLE BOOK WHERE I WOULD BLOT OUT HIS LOATHSOME MEMORY FOR EVER. YOU SEE, THE ONLY POSSIBLE JOY ONE COULD ACHIEVE IN A DREARY MENSWEAR SHOP WAS THE CONTACT WITH INTERESTING PEOPLE WHO MIGHT COME IN . . . THEY WERE MY ESCAPE. IT WAS A SHOP FOR THE RICHER

CUSTOMERS WHO WANTED THEIR SHIRTS MADE, AND WAS RUN BY A VERY LOVABLE GENTLEMAN CALLED HARRY FISHER. SO IT WAS A SHIRTMAKER'S CALLED *FISHER*, BUT NOW, ALAS, NO LONGER THERE. OLD HARRY WOULD LEAN OVER THE COUNTER WAITING FOR TRADE, AND SMOKE MANIKIN CIGARS WHICH WOULD LEAVE A NICE PUNGENT SMELL IN THE SHOP, AND OCCASIONALLY OLD HARRY WOULD SHARE HIS LUNCH WITH ME WHICH WAS VERY NICE AND JUST AS GOOD AS MY MUM'S.

So there I was with notebook, because it was either that or go mad and give the game away: punch this manager in the face or hold on to my job. Go raving mad and run the King through and no one will believe me but put it down to thwarted ambition. On some occasions I didn't use the book but opted out along with the others and merely used my hands against my forehead – the heels of my hands – and said *My tables* – i.e. my memory, soul and mind. But this is a cop-out. I dropped the book once in another scene and felt a right slob. I don't admire actors who are always dropping things on stage because they are uncentred and because the whole audience inwardly winces and the scene is temporarily blurred by this piece of distraction. So I left the book out on a subsequent production, but now it was in and I took it carefully out and wrote, *So, uncle, there you are.* I would point directly to my skull as if I had him trapped in there. Trapped him in the soup of revenge that would stew him.

Hamlet has already called his skull his distracted globe, so now and again it could also be his notebook. When Plummer did it he wrote in the dirt with his sword. I suppose a lot of actors feel daft at that moment actually taking out a little notebook. Some actors have a book hanging round their necks and tucked into their doublet which they whip out like the milkman taking orders. But it is the carefulness and method of Hamlet which they ignore by writing on the air or in the dirt. I believe Olivier wrote it down. Let us obey Shakespeare and he will not lead us astray. So when he says write, you may be sure that if you do this there will come some other gems that will fit in.

Hamlet　　　　　　　　**Now, to my Word,**

45

> It is 'Adieu, adieu, remember me.'
> I have sworn't.

(I didn't pray though.) He looks down at the stage floor and his friends Horatio and Marcellus call from below. He is high above them and can see them.

> Come, bird, come.

If they were only birds they could fly right to him, so much does he want to impart his news. Good news. They fly across the stage. Hamlet flies to meet them . . . they miss each other and wheel around . . . they are across the stage, a little distance from him . . .

> *Horatio* **What news, my lord?**

Urgent, bursting, tell us. I want to tell everything, but suddenly I think not, I'm cautious suddenly.

> *Hamlet* **O, wonderful!**

Light and sarcastic almost – as if nothing much happened, old boy – almost mincing; after the passion and the run, a deliberate piece of trickery.

> *Horatio* **Good my lord, tell it.**

I.e. 'Don't piss about, let us in.' Their passion and his coolness are now in total contrast to the prior scene when the fools tried to hold him back. Fools. I wouldn't have found all this out if I had listened to their cautions.

> *Hamlet* **No,**

A bit petulant . . . a pause . . .

> **you will reveal it.**

Now I am in possession of the real facts I shall hold on to them. Now I am so excited to have found out the truth, to have spoken to my father, to be given such a cause, to have such a weight of responsibility – that I can no longer reason. I play games since I cannot bring myself to tell them the simple truth. I cannot trust them.

> *Hamlet* **There's never a villain dwelling in all Denmark**
> **But he's an arrant knave.**

A little hint. It is a court card and the lowest. Claudius is the lowest scoundrel in the court. Then I speedily go about my business like one in a frenzy, taking the next lines at a pace. I have to get away. These people are too slow; therefore I cannot and will not trust them. Although my hint was a touch too clever.

> *Horatio*   **There needs no ghost, my lord, come from the grave**
> **To tell us this.**
>
> *Hamlet*   **Why, right, you are in the right.**

He gets a bit precious here:

> **I will go pray.**

This last line is a trifle priggish and middle class. It is also rather dismissive of the men who have been watching on the cold, blustering night – who have told him everything. The least a decent man would do would be to tell and confide, but suddenly these are ordinary mortals whereas Hamlet has spoken with the dead. Hamlet even deliberately misreads Horatio's words to provide himself with wit, when Horatio humbly says there's *no offence* after Hamlet's half-hearted apology, for his *wild and whirling words*:

> *Hamlet*   **I am sorry they offend you, heartily –**
> **Yes faith, heartily.**
>
> *Horatio*   **There's no offence, my lord.**
>
> *Hamlet*   **Yes by Saint Patrick, but there is . . .**

and then reveals it is an honest ghost, but reveals no more.

An honest ghost. I suppose Hamlet must be bound to secrecy since he is the only one trusted with the message and the task. To tell would dilute.

> *Hamlet*   **For your desire to know what is between us,**
> **O'ermaster't as you may.**

Superior and royal – you can act this as gentle as you like but the meaning is clear. It means – perhaps even unconsciously – Put that in your pipe and smoke it. Hamlet suddenly becomes rather remote and superior. A little flattery now:

> *Hamlet*   **As you are friends, scholars, and soldiers,**
> **Give me one poor request.**

And then asks them to say nothing when in fact they know next to nothing anyway. His dismissive attitude towards his informants is scurrilous and cavalier and quite out of character. So what did I do? I cut it. And it runs quite well and more feelingly to go straight to:

> **Touching this vision here,**
> **It is an honest ghost . . .**

Straight, hard, bald fact. Give them something; they have been shivering in the cold for two hours or so – four if we think of twelve o'clock striking at the entrance of the Ghost and the glow-worm showing the matin to be near.

Something lovely about the dawning of a new day . . . at the beginning of dawn our figures are seen swearing an oath never to repeat what we have seen tonight. The Ghost reinforces it. We make a strange sight, this group of people racing over the ground being pursued by a ghost working his way through the earth. The chorus picks up the sound of *swear* and it vibrates around the building. We move again.

Horatio **O day and night, but this is wondrous strange.**
Hamlet **And therefore as a stranger give it welcome.**

Now the antic scene must be played slow. Suddenly he is revealing the way he will operate from now on. We are conspirators. Now I spell it out, clearly and succinctly, for the audience must understand what *antic disposition* means. You know – a little gesture to the head to subtly inform those who don't quite get it, and the responding laugh shows that now they do, so you have mined and cleaned up an old gem. Although now he elaborates: I shall act the loony so don't give me away. A split-second flash of a loony since I also am enjoying relishing the role. The Ghost again utters *Swear* as the chorus joins in a slow falling-away echo that seems to fade across a long distance. I do something naughty now, but this is the time for such things. In the depth of tragedy there can be a mad humour. The Ghost has now been continually demanding *swear* – four times in fact – and so, just in a friendly familiar way, I knock on the stage with my fist and say *Rest*, as if requesting a noisy neighbour to pipe down. Then add, *perturbed spirit*. Shocking place to get a laugh, I know, but I think that it can be justified since Hamlet's mind is already unhinged by the experience and in his present euphoria he might well even play with death.

Then we cut the speech, *So, gentlemen, / With all my love I do*

48

commend me to you. Suddenly Hamlet is humble, noble, concerned, when he has just more or less said, 'Do as I say, maggots, and I'll tell you precisely nothing . . . be kept in the dark.' This crumbling into a heap of obsequious nonsense is best left out. *And what so poor a man as Hamlet*, etc. – put a sock in it, mate. Perhaps this is the way I see it. With a gentle reading it can overcome the qualities I have read into it, too much false humility and princely largesse. I never like it when powerful people suddenly behave like helpless little cogs in a big machine.

But we go offstage, or off to the side. The actors are still sitting stage right in the line, and I am walking backwards saying, *Let's go together*. We are on the north side and we take a right-angle and go to join the line. I sit at the end of the line. The scene then dissolves into:

ACT II

SCENE I

A room in the house of Polonius.

We have cut the nasty little scene of Polonius's further obsession with sex and games when he actually sends a spy to Paris. It's boring and unnecessary and was put there so that the audience will feel that enough time has passed for Hamlet to have performed the events that Ophelia describes.

As I sit Ophelia screams and dashes on stage, circling the perimeter of the stage is if down a long corridor, arriving in the arms of Polonius who has taken his time while she is camouflaging his entrance with her run. Consequently, she flies into his stationary being as if he had always been there. The next, I stole from Olivier: it fitted so well into our style and also neatly doubled the action, so Hamlet could be seen doing what she describes. An audience is naturally apt to see things that follow each other as being in sequence – even if they know they are not – since we live in sequence and without jumps; it is a natural biological and psychological fact.

Ophelia   **O my lord, I have been so affrighted.**

During her speech I enter the stage and mime if you like – but really counterpoint the action – putting the actual events in the minds of the audience.

Now why do this and not let the words convey it? They do and apart from the time sequence I have mentioned the mime actually adds another dimension to the scene. The actor is a vehicle for the words, but in this situation I felt that the image would enrich the audience's perception of the scene, in the way Olivier did in his film. I have never forgotten the image of him going into Ophelia's closet and doing this, though I have long forgotten Ophelia's rendering of the lines. So much stage action is starved of visual heightening, and the audience's senses can become starved as much

53

by an abundance of language as by an absence of sensual and visual stimulation.

O my lord, my lord, I have been so affrighted.

She starts her speech and in the meantime I have dishevelled myself and create the very image that she now sees. She meanwhile acts out the sewing in her closet and Polonius stands there listening. He says the lines to her while I am actually doing the scene and taking her by the wrist, etc. – but of course he doesn't see me since he is in present time and I am in past. It worked very well. I am pretending to be mad since I know that she will report this immediately, which of course she does.

We must assume that Hamlet has known that Ophelia has betrayed or might betray him, for him to take this course of action. Or we can assume the opposite: that Hamlet has come to tell her that he can no longer countenance the love they had since he now has a murder to commit, and looks at her with deep regret and leaves with a huge sigh, signifying the end of love for both of them. But since Hamlet's behaviour seems so clear just after he has seen the Ghost, I took the opposite point of view: that he was using her as bait. Therefore I acted mad for her. I acted the loony, putting the antic disposition on since this is the scene most apt for a trial demonstration. There is little demonstration actually in the play of any particularly strange behaviour – except for a bit of fun with Polonius. For the rest of the time Hamlet is extremely sane, courteous and reasonable. The audience, seeing me with my socks round my ankles and acting rather strangely, found this to be very funny, and in their eyes there was no mistaking what I was trying to do. Ophelia's speech, then, was less about a love- or tragedy-struck Hamlet than about a calculating or devious one who is setting in motion his feigned madness. After all, she has returned his letters and refused to see him – obviously obeying the commands of others – so my actions will let those 'others' know what I am up to.

It works. Polonius judges that I am mad and thus it will go straight to the ear of the King and Queen. Well done. As Polonius and

Ophelia exit John Prior plays a slow march in a court-music style, and the actors walk in time to the music and adjust their places. The King and Queen are now on stage left, and Polonius, Ophelia and Hamlet, plus others, are upstage in a line. The Ghost, now an actor, pushes two chairs which slowly scrape a whining howl against the wooden floor and he adjusts himself and moves back to the lines as a court servant.

SCENE II

Rosencrantz and Guildenstern.

The flourish created a sequence that we made much use of. The flourish and business of the court also affords the possibility of changing the scene. It clears the air and new energy is about to be used. Matthew Scurfield, as Claudius, sits ready and waiting. David and Tony Meyer are twins; so cast for this very reason, but also they are very very good indeed as Rosencrantz and Guildenstern. But it helped the confusion of identities. They bow and scrape their way on after the King has uttered his welcoming line, each one trying to outdo the other in the stakes for abject fawning and sycophantic arse-licking.

The twins were at first reluctant to work with each other since they felt their individual merits were either lost or compromised by each other's effect. They were naturally individuals and anxious about any slur that might be cast on their ability to work without the other. On the other hand, as Rosencrantz and Guildenstern it suited the situation rather well and created an added theatricality while allowing more devious confusions to arise. I had worked with one of the twins, Tony Meyer, in my adaptation of *The Trial*, by Kafka, several years earlier. He was inventive and quick. The other twin, David, had a harder and more serious face. But although together there was no confusing who they were, when they were apart one might deny the identity of one by calling him by his brother's name. However, they were a joy to work with and both looked very polished, handsome and Oxbridge.

The King now puts to them the reason for their visit, which is not only one of spreading a little good cheer, but yet another spying role. There are more spies here than in MI5. Each commissioner of the spy believing that the cause is good and worthy, each justifying the intrusion as being for the welfare of the state. Everyone is doing it to everyone else. Then the Queen goes on to make her little speech, thus reinforcing basically what Claudius has already said, and adding her two-penny worth since she is on the stage and Shakespeare reckoned that she should perhaps show the more thankful and generous side of the duo. Rosencrantz and Guildenstern answer as unctuously as they possibly can. After all, they are suddenly promoted to do a service for a king by this stroke of luck.

I will not expand on this scene since I am really Hamlet and am not here when it is taking place. I can really relate only to my own part in the main while reflecting on the others in passing – what I see, overhear, or spy on, like everyone else. Rosencrantz and Guilden-stern go off. As they do they turn and become the double doors that Polonius goes through. Thus we establish the chamber of the King and Queen. Music covers their retreat and Polonius comes on through the doors. The King and Queen have snuggled up and are groping on the couch (two chairs). Ah for a bit of passion after all this court business, and Claudius is not too particular where he does it. So while he is groping Gertrude, Polonius coughs politely, which eventually turns into a loud bark.

Polonius coughs ridiculously loudly and the King and Queen sit up and pay attention. David Auker's performance is totally unlike the usual doddering Polonius. We are so used to the white-haired old fool that we are apt to turn off when he comes in. So, in this case, the obese, sweating and primping Polonius belongs to another character which we may have borrowed to throw the original into greater relief. With his greasy, parted-in-the-centre hair and silly moustache he stands waiting for the attention of the King. The court becomes a slow ritual. The drum ticks out the rhythm of an old grandfather clock. Polonius walks to the rhythm. The chorus is waiting and watching and becomes a jury listening to the evidence as Polonius slowly unravels his case. He is the lawyer and the cast a jury following his movement across the stage. It is slow and hypnotic. Polonius begins his speech.

We had great difficulty making this scene work at first, but eventually it was very interesting to see how we had transformed the scene into something quite intense. I imagined the great grandfather clock ticking away and a huge fireplace. I could see Claudius sitting with a pair of huge dogs, half bloated and mildly snarling and being shushed by the King. Or the heavy clock beating out its relentless time against a dull leaden sky, and Polonius in the background walking and gesticulating. So this is how I imagined it might be if I were filming it . . . in almost every scene I saw a film when the atmosphere was intense, and in other places there was no filmic image at all – only what we had created on stage.

Polonius gives out his information as though he were giving away little Christmas parcels, clinging to them and then letting them go like little treasures he is doling out to children. Now, as the layers are slowly stripped away, he reveals a strategy; no more bumbling Polonius tripping over words, but a shrewd politician and lawyer; a sharp, sweaty, clever lawyer, building up the tension from the word *expostulate*, biting on the end of the word to grab attention and taking his time as he draws on the words like a smoker drawing on a good cigar. He builds up to the climax which for him is:

Polonius　**Your noble son is mad.**

Ophelia and I are sitting on the stage next to each other, as if on trial; in effect we are, if only in their mind's eye. So we are sitting there, sometimes holding each other's hands as we are humiliated in the public scourging and mockery. You might say that we are in the stocks. Polonius continues like an orator spelling out every possible nuance and titillating the 'jury'. He shows the letter – mimed, of course, which allows for some elaborate unfolding and shaking out of the document. He reads the letter, but in a mocking way and causes everybody to laugh after the King, in relief, gives the cue with a forced joviality:

Polonius **In her excellent white bosom, these, etc.**

The King is relieved . . . oh ho ho . . . is this all? . . . there is indeed nothing to worry about. It is only love, not bloody revenge for usurping the throne from Hamlet, which is the red herring. The whole court feels that Hamlet's peevishness and low mien are due more to the fact that Claudius took over the reins of the country instead of him.

Polonius . . . **whilst this machine is to him, Hamlet.**

Now the King echoes the word *machine*. We all think this word is very funny, and prevent Polonius from continuing while he delights himself with the absurd sound of *machine*. The whole court laughs now out loud at the adolescent love being sent up so mercilessly while Hamlet and Ophelia by contrast do nothing except sit with the utmost calm and dignity. The King then asks Polonius how she has received Hamlet's love.

Since Hamlet and Ophelia are on the stage being the image in the mind's eye of the audience, we are now able to flash back to the events. She is pulled jerkily out of the line by her father and abjectly treated while Polonius shows how he did *bespeak* . . . and goes on to tell her:

Polonius **Lord Hamlet is a prince out of thy star.**

Scolding her, while the court is now watching in its 'mind's eye' as we dovetail the two times. She meanwhile is seen pleading with her father and is dismissed. Now he comes over to me and drags me out as witness number two in court. And while he is mocking me I am acting out the various descriptions that he provides:

Polonius **And he, repelled . . .**

> **Fell into sadness, then into a fast,**
> **Thence to a watch, thence into a weakness,**
> **Thence to a lightness, and, by this declension,**
> **Into the madness wherein now he raves . . .**

Now this is not illustrating; rather it is satirizing. While we are acting out sequences we are also able to change the monotonous linear sequence that has the audience anticipating. This pulls them up with a jolt and wakes them because the mind travels backwards and forwards. I think the reason a lot of people fall asleep in the theatre is because it is a similar experience to travelling in a train and seeing the country unfolding; you are able to fall asleep because the mind acclimatizes itself to the sequential nature of things. The brain is used to problems out of sequence. Every drama as it is happening in real life does not unfold so neatly as the play that describes the events. So, when Joseph K is being arrested in Kafka's *The Trial*, we see the laundry hanging out on the sill. This detail becomes almost as important as the arrest in artistic terms, since we are thrown backwards and forwards in time and significance. Things rarely happen so neatly, and when they do there is a revolt because the brain is adjusted to think on multi-levels in order to survive. And when one goes to the theatre several of the attentive levels either rebel or become obsessed in other problems so that the play becomes background and is picked up, so to speak, by the only channel that can be bothered to receive it; or there is simply not enough information coming in to prevent the brain from starving and then escaping through sleep. Film can beat this problem by constantly changing your point of view so that your mind or eye is made to travel in a split second to another face. If you turn away you might easily miss a whole new image. Added to this, music works away at the sensory mechanism, thus underlining and reinforcing the events, and thus there is no way that a thrilling film can bore you. It may also enthrall you by working full out on all the channels of your receptivity.

In the theatre we are left with the static, boring image which causes the oxygen to leave the brain since the brain is not being used. The director has no idea of the responsibility he has towards the amazingly overtuned twentieth-century mind. He thinks of all theatre as literature anyway (which he doesn't realize is highly symbolic, since one reads at night after work, or in bed, and creates the most wonderful images of one's own). Now on the stage you are provided with the visible image of the man or woman and are thus robbed of

59

the possibility of making your own image up. Therefore the director has the responsibility of creating images and moods that are better than, or as good as, those in one's mind. Instead, they are frequently duller, at least the ones I have seen in Britain. By this I mean even the images conjured up in the voices of the actors. Even a lean and spare production can excite by the emotional power of the actors, so I am not suggesting an elaborate *mise-en-scène*. I am talking here purely about the staging and visualization of an event. Now a young mind is working at many more levels than an older, tired mind, and the reason young people hate going to the theatre is less to do with cultural ignorance than the imaginative ignorance of the director. And when one creates a *mise-en-scène* which is imaginative or recognizes the wandering mind of the spectator, the production is curiously called 'European'. Here in England we are used to a kind of dullness . . . a safe representational and 'natural' reading.

So, in this scene, I have used this example to illustrate simply how we are able to engage the mind on another level by showing the point of view of the characters who are not supposed to be on stage.

Polonius pulls me on to the stage and I fall into *a sadness*, but I use the event further to play the madness of Hamlet and to ridicule the descriptions. The audience laughs and the scene demonstrates for Polonius his success – that Hamlet is stupid and a bit crazy. I return to the seat and join Ophelia. The King asks:

King **How may we try it further?**

The piano is now playing a simple tune while the others are acting or thinking of how they may do this. They agree to a plan, and when the Queen says:

Queen **But look where sadly the poor wretch comes reading.**
I am coming on.

The music plays now a furtive tune which invites a kind of *danse macabre* as the actors tiptoe out in time to the music and hide. I come on reading a large book and, of course, know well that I am being spied on. I have pulled one or both trouser legs up above my knees, wear crazy specs, and slowly walk on, crouched over the book. I do look rather strange. I mean, I look a mess. The King and Gertrude hide behind the chairs on stage left while the others are on stage right, all peeking through, much like a family party playing a children's game of spying or peek-a-boo. I walk slowly on, my face hidden by the huge book I am carrying, while impersonating a nutty professor.

Polonius **How does my good Lord Hamlet?**

My face slowly rises over the book, like a moon, totally vacant.

Hamlet **Well, God-a-mercy.**

I smile the idiot's grin and dip back into my book.

Polonius **Do you know me, my lord?**

I sniff around a bit, and then recognize an unsavoury whiff.

Hamlet **Excellent well. You are a fishmonger.**

We carry on the familiar banter:

Hamlet **For if the sun breed maggots in a dead dog, being a good kissing carrion . . .**

Does this mean that even Polonius as a piece of dead carrion can breed a daughter? So is he like a dead dog and can Ophelia be in Hamlet's mind like maggots? Sometimes it is best not to know or to take no special tack, but make the line clear and let the audience take it the way they wish, so I let them interpret this. All this goes over Polonius's head, but to make the meaning clear for me and the audience I play it grossly and leeringly:

Hamlet **– Have you a daughter?**

Eyebrows leaping up and down on my face and winking like a Soho pimp trying to sell a piece of flesh. For that is what Polonius is – a pimp – making his daughter walk the streets for me as the bait for the fish. Polonius the ponce, flogging off the helpless piece of flesh.

The scene raised a huge laugh, as Shakespeare does when the audience is seeing something contemporaneous in the text and the action. Again, I am influenced by the Guthrie–Plummer *Hamlet*, so rich in invention that I steal some choice bits – and my respects to Christopher Plummer:

Polonius **What do you read, my lord?**

Such a set-up.

Hamlet **Words, words, words.**

Here Plummer shook the book as if the words would fall out and thus

61

show themselves as evidence and so, as I am much tempted to little displays of parody or a kind of physical satire, I would listen to the book, putting it to my ear as a kind of ancient cassette deck, or I would shake the words out of the book like Plummer, and sometimes I would go a bit madder and shake the words out and pick one off the floor and pretend I held it there between my finger and thumb: a tiny little word hanging there.

Polonius refers to the King and Queen behind the chairs, nipping back and forth while I continue my strange walk. I feel most justified in anything here, since Hamlet is proving himself mad and there is a certain amount of licence I feel I can give myself.

Polonius **What is the matter, my lord?**
Another awful and easy set-up.

Hamlet **Between who?**
I look startled and ready to flee in fear. I then round on him on,

> **Slanders, sir; for the satirical rogue says here that old men have grey beards**

and the list corresponds with my scrutiny of his face as I say the lines and check them off against the thing in front of me.

At the end, after that skilful last banter,

> **You cannot, sir, take from me anything that I will not more willingly part withal – except my life, except my life, except my life.**

I took it into my head to mime a chicken or rooster, which seemed to grow out of my stance and voice, and with wings flaying and flapping I clucked him off the stage. Now what a crazy idea. I didn't feel too good about it at first, though it got many laughs. Matthew Scurfield was reading a copy of *Hamlet* out of the many editions that were floating around and I cannot remember which one it was, but it described an event, perhaps in an early version of the play, when Hamlet in his madness feigns a cockerel. I thought this was a fairly brave and extraordinary thing to do. Now in acting you can go over the top and be an embarrassment, but with a little conviction and not a little bravery you can not only get away with it but create quite a dangerous impression of a man who will go to any lengths to achieve his end. This scene was nearly always successful, especially in Europe when we played the second and third leg of our tour. It was fun to do and created a relief for the audience. Perhaps in some ways I was influenced by Plummer because his business was so damn daring and witty that he made any Hamlet following him look wooden. Plummer soared and was quite the best Hamlet for me. So much did he influence me, that two years later, in 1965, when performing in *Zoo Story* at Stratford East, I tried to express the very daring and openness that he could demonstrate, from power to extraordinary tenderness. In *Zoo Story* I had unlocked a way of seeing character and let it fill my whole body. I felt I had captured a certain technique from watching Plummer for those six valuable weeks of my life, and my reviews from *Zoo Story* were quite the best I have had – then or ever. Plummer taught me to fly. So perhaps I didn't always fly, but I shall always try to remember the huge passion which was not just vocal and emotional but an intelligent and caustic passion. But, my God, the daring . . . the supreme and utter leaps of the imagination. Only Olivier rivalled him, and, out of all the Hamlets I have seen, his was one of the best.

So I clucked Polonius off the stage, and I think if you saw a grown and intelligent man who was not drunk you might find him quite dangerous in that situation. It means at the same time that Hamlet is unpredictable, and that spells danger.

Rosencrantz and Guildenstern.

Polonius races off downstage; music plays, and I find myself greeting Rosencrantz and Guildenstern at the opposite ends of the diagonal. I have, during this last scene change, adjusted my dress and tucked my shirt in, and the cast has rearranged itself to suggest the change of scene. The music accentuates the change and everybody moves to the sound; as the music stops, I confront them. The music is quite important in the swift changes of scene that take place: it suggests the wiping out of the prior scene and, when the music suddenly stops, attention to the new scene before us.

Trying to be suitably bonkers

Bob Hornery (as Polonius), whose expression seems to be saying, 'Well, even if it's what they call Experimental Theatre, at least they do pay Equity rates.'

There are so many ways of greeting old friends. There they are, smiling and expectant.

    Hamlet   **My excellent good friends . . .**

I start. Then, of course, I trade on the confusion:

    Guildenstern? Ah, Rosencrantz.

Slightly unsure which hand belongs to which name and, after some readjustment of handshakes, I say:

    Good lads . . .

Anyway, it doesn't matter.

    . . . how do you both?

The joke of course came with the strong emphasis on *My excellent good friends* and then forgetting who is which.

  We are treading a tight path and still on the diagonal. They come close to me – there is some awkwardness. It is all spoken quite deliberately and slowly, like ex-public schoolboys trying to recapture some of the carefree banter that we had and really no longer have; the forced joviality that characterizes awkwardness. We banter on and, like dirty schoolboys, soon get into a bit of filth:

    Guildenstern   **Faith, her privates we.**

Rosencrantz significantly lifts up the back of his coat and I perform a brief mime of schoolboy vulgarity. 'Oooh!'

    Hamlet   **In the secret parts of Fortune? O most true,**
                 she is a strumpet.

Lots of giggles, followed by a hollow silence as they and I look awkwardly at each other and smile in a sheepish way. They stand with hands behind their backs waiting for the next move, and I let them stew in their discomfort for a while before deciding to break with:

    Hamlet   **What news?**

I.e., 'What are you doing here?' Rosencrantz gives me a stupid answer, which of course is another of Shakespeare's set-ups for a pithy aphorism.

    Rosencrantz   **None, my lord, but the world's grown honest.**
    Hamlet   **Then is doomsday near.**

I put my arms around them and go for a little walk downstage on the diagonal.

Hamlet   **But your news is not true. Let me question more in particular. What have you, my good friends, deserved at the hands of Fortune that she sends you to prison hither?**

Guildenstern   **Prison, my lord?**

Hamlet   **Denmark's a prison.**

I say this honestly and feelingly, and with a sense of wishing to confide in them. I need them to be honest and rely on it – as if they may say, 'We agree', or 'I know what you mean', or anything, in the way that Horatio says:

Horatio   **Indeed, my lord, it follow'd hard upon.** [I, ii]

But no such honesty is to come out of their mouths. No.

Rosencrantz   **Then is the world one.**

– as if the world could be like this, and this is just as good as anywhere else you could name. Like people who always say (and know nothing else), 'This is the best country to live in.' So I have to reinforce my statement to get at least some measure of discontent – some radical word, some little howl of protest to show some degree of spirit. But no:

Rosencrantz   **We think not so, my lord.**

Hamlet   **Why, then 'tis none to you; for there is nothing either good or bad but thinking makes it so. To me it is a prison.**

Maybe the dogs can now follow my train of thought – that I am the one stuck in this abominable situation. But no, again everything is hunkydory:

Rosencrantz   **Why, then your ambition makes it one: 'tis too narrow for your mind.**

Like my mind, they retort; my ambition makes it one – as if I am not satisfied with life that is so abundant to them.

Hamlet   **O God . . .**

I answer as if to say, 'Oh, what a bloody stupid, boring and obvious piece of sophistry. Oh God!' – as if this is what I have to contend with. I take the words *O God* away from the next sentence and let them hang in the air, smelling of my contempt:

Hamlet **I could be bounded in a nutshell and count myself
a king of infinite space – were it not that I have
bad dreams.**

But I am finding this all too boring and want to get out of here. Let's change the scene.

Hamlet **Shall we to th' court? For by my fay, I cannot reason.**

I.e., 'I can't talk to idiots.' We walk down as they say:

Rosencrantz and Guildenstern **We'll wait upon you.**

I.e., 'We'll go with you.' My interpretation: they are waiters or servants sent by the King to pick up the crumbs from the table. So insultingly I misinterpret:

Hamlet **No such matter. I will not sort you with the rest
of my servants; for, to speak to you like an honest
man, I am most dreadfully attended.**

I am saying that my staff or retinue is very small at the present time, and I let them open the door for me. In fact I change them into a pair of doors and go through them.

We turn on stage and then, as if going into another room, I open the doors and walk a little ahead, saying as I walk:

Hamlet **But** (*very casual now*) **in the beaten way of friendship,
what make you at Elsinore?**

Rosencrantz **To visit you, my lord, no other occasion.**

Hamlet **Beggar that I am, I am even poor in thanks,
but I thank you. And sure, dear friends, my thanks
are too dear a halfpenny.**

So forgetful of me not to be thankful to you . . . so have my cheap thanks.

Then, as I am walking ahead I casually turn and say, just dropping it into their laps:

Hamlet **Were you not sent for?**

So lightly, like a soufflé, nothing too heady in it, adding: 'Hmmmm?' – Come on, chaps,

Is it your own inclining?

Still a bit light and jokey:

Is it a free visitation?

They can't speak. The question is too direct and unexpected, too frank and ruthless, and there I stand just looking at them and bearing down on them, but still resisting the temptation to blast out:

Come, come. Nay, speak.

Shouted out as I did at first, but now a little more lingering; dipping the words in an acid bath is better. Still over-gentle, as if reproving a child:

Hamlet **You were sent for . . .**

Like, 'I caught you out', spinning out the vowels like a child winning a game. I've got the wind on them. Giggles from both of them and blushes, if that were possible:

> **. . . there is a kind of confession in your looks, which your modesties have not craft enough to colour.**

Shaping my hand over my face as if I could read the face with the palm; or even sometimes taking the cheeks as if reproving a naughty child.

> **I know the good King and Queen have sent for you.**

Again, I've caught them out. I do this with a little beckoning of my forefinger, like a superior summoning two slaves.

They are chameleons who reflect the world that they are in. So, while obviously not corrupt, they are made so by their own lack of colour, which makes them take on any stronger hue in the way that weak characters take on the fashion and greed of the time. Hamlet stands out in his black, which symbolizes at the same time his unwillingness to blend into the grey conformist world of the others. At university this may not have been so apparent to Hamlet, since they were not challenged in beliefs or principles by power, which seems to corrupt by draining all into the general mode. In the same way the uniforms of an army have to be identical in order to distinguish it from the enemy. At the same time the uniforms are very symbolic: you are burying yourself in the attitude of the mob.

So they were sent for . . .

Rosencrantz **To what end, my lord?**

What on earth can you be thinking?

Hamlet **That, you must teach me.**

If you're the one who knows, how can I tell you what you have already been told by others? So much better to go straight to:

> **. . . be even and direct with me whether you were sent for or no.**

Now firmer . . . Come one, let's not piss about . . . You are forced to be a liar, because I have given you no option . . . Yes or no? They go to one side and I walk away to save them the embarrassment. They return with beaming faces to assuage their perfidy, as if, all right, mate, the game's up, but you know how it is:

> *Guildenstern* **My lord, we were . . . sent for.**

Then straight and hard:

> *Hamlet* **I will tell you why . . .**

So you needn't look any further –

> **. . . so shall my anticipation prevent your discovery, and your secrecy to the King and Queen moult no feather.**

A lovely image. All actors have bits of biz that they like to do to redesign a line, and so I took the invisible feather between finger and thumb and let it float down, and then caught it as it softly fell into the crook of my other palm.

The next lines I did lightly, almost thrown away but not quite, almost in parentheses. Not too serious . . . not yet. But I would increase the volume slowly, like a man becoming possessed with an idea. If I let myself flow with it and relax, it would start to ignite slowly by the time I came to

> **. . . this most excellent canopy the air, look you . . .**
> **this . . . brave . . . o'erhanging firmament . . . this**
> (*and now very slowly, letting the sounds and the words take hold*) **majestical roof fretted with golden fire . . .**

To do this I would let myself become, if you like, weak, so that I could control as little as possible and it would take hold of me until I could climb a crescendo without appearing to strain. I tried to reach a high as if to score a hit, the words becoming the drug that would take me with them. This is one of the few speeches I could do this with. To flow with it; otherwise it would appear stultified and forced. And if I tried to reproduce it naturally I would find myself shouting as if to

appear (except to those who know) that it has ended . . . and then you continue and then it appears to stop . . . and then you go on to the end. So many actors do speeches and you know when they have come to the end of a line that there is more to come, because they do not rest to let the thoughts arise in the brain – with them the thoughts are there all the time and are even curdling the lines before and after. Alec McCowen, a great Shakespearian actor, always made me feel that he was making the lines up as he went along. He was so fresh and spontaneous and his whole body would be in his voice and words; his body was a tight nerve, or rather pipeline, of energy, carrying the force of the line with him – the way the main artery of the body feeds the minor ones. So he would feed every tributary and colour every nuance in his speech. He was a fine teacher: Malvolio, Mercutio, Dauphin, Fool in *King Lear*, Dromio, etc., etc. I think you can learn more from watching great actors than can ever be taught in drama school and I think – since acting is based on observation – that there could be no better way of learning than to watch the greats.

Now I cannot go to the theatre because I believe that there has been a conspiracy by directors to steal the limelight; that they fear somehow the vast armoury of the actor that would make an audience cringe in fear and delight. The directors want to be seen and to be seen to be seen. The great actors have gone – their ways are too idiosyncratic. They are the true aristocrats and they have been banned. I cannot account otherwise for the sheer paucity of the huge playing we used to have in the days of the actor–manager when the actors were the stars. Productions may have been poorer, but it was still possible to have good directors like Tyrone Guthrie, Glen Byam Shaw, Michel Saint-Denis and Peter Brook, and still keep the integrity of a thought-out production with a towering performance. Now we have respectable actors, which I approve of, but also a coterie of yes-men directors who work with the company style. It is possible that I have not seen great acting on the English stage for ten years, and the last time was Olivier in *Othello*. I think Brook, in his further investigation into theatrical art, has probably killed off more actors than anyone, but made of some ordinary actors quite good ones – not great ones because nobody is allowed to be greater than Brook. However, I would go to a Brook production over any others at any time. But now I am as Hamlet defending the territory of the actor, and his territory has been usurped by the conglomerates. The large companies' biggest successes are interestingly enough the non-actors' plays – adaptations of Dickens or musicals based on T. S. Eliot's poems. They have successfully crushed the actor out of existence; they have promoted reasonable actors but no one of awesome power – not an Olivier, an Irving, a Kean, or even a ——— – if they looked like becoming stars they would mysteriously disappear. Anyway, I still believe that Shakespeare wrote great arias – the equivalent of operatic arias – and that a man played Shakespeare all his life or a good part of it. Opera has its Domingos, Callases, Sutherlands. Where are the theatre's sacred monsters?

Rosencrantz and Guildenstern cannot speak so I continue:

Hamlet   **Man delights not me – nor woman neither, though by your smiling you seem to say so.**

My pay-off almost for the whole speech really has been:

   . . . **yet, to me, what is this quintessence of dust?**

I come back to this. I implore them for an answer. What is this for? I try to squeeze it out of them. What are we doing on this earth? Why are we suffering so much? They are left in the limbo of their own cowardice and ignorance – their own fear of coming to terms with what a man is – and will probably vote Tory next time.

Rosencrantz   **My lord, there was no such stuff in my thoughts.**

Hamlet   . . . **what is this quintessence of dust?**

I strike and examine myself. What am I? What is my purpose? There must be some reason. I have played this scene as one who is, or might be, mad or highly strung, but clear with the clarity and purpose that we often find in the loonies who get obsessed with one idea and let nothing else clutter it – unlike most people who talk and at the same time have a cross-current of a thousand other thoughts nagging and conflicting while speaking only the tip of the iceberg of the real thought and meaning. In this speech it is direct, clean and sharp. It is a lesson:

> **Man delights not me –**

Rosencrantz and Guildenstern smile . . .

> **nor woman neither,**

They smile again . . .

> **though by your smiling you seem to say so.**

We know that I mean mankind in general. Am I making a slight semantic joke here – *nor woman neither* – or am I really saying that their tendentious interpretation of *Man* makes me defend myself perhaps from some little secret they all shared at university – Shakespeare also. We are always hearing – from homosexuals especially – that Shakespeare was a gay. He married and had a family so he could have been bisexual. So is this little secret of *Man delights not me* deliberately misconstrued to mean, 'The male delights not me'? But then they say:

> *Rosencrantz* . . . **if you delight not in man, what Lenten entertainment the players shall receive from you.**

Rosencrantz and Guildenstern have merely smiled – insinuatingly – and it is Shakespeare who has put the thought (dangerous as well in those times) in their heads. A small joke from the 'others'. Rosencrantz and Guildenstern gabble their way out of the situation with their introduction of the players which enables them to twist away from the smiling innuendo. Now Shakespeare could not say *Man delights not me . . . though by your smiling you seem to say so*, and leave out *nor woman neither* since this would clearly imply some shared knowledge of homosexuality. So the *woman neither* is a camouflage or smokescreen. Shakespeare obviously has little time for women and spends all his time with men. His players are all male and the young ones play women; how tender it must have been to see a young boy playing Juliet, or Desdemona, or Rosalind especially. What a delightful confusion. Perhaps there is a hint here of Hamlet's love for men which they know of. His passion for Horatio is clear and platonic; or is it . . . ?

> *Hamlet*   **Give me that man**

That is not passion's slave, and I will wear him
In my heart's core, ay, in my heart of heart,
As I do thee. [III, ii]

Rather fulsome, even to a good friend, but add:

Something too much of this.

Too much of what? Grand sexual passion? – or merely something too much of my gushing, old boy . . . bit sentimental, what? Something too much of what? We are used to frank confessions, so I may be saying I mustn't allow my emotions to cloud the issue that faces us at the moment.

But Shakespeare leaves a lot of clues to his woman-hatred dotted around. As Hamlet to Ophelia:

God hath given you one face and you make yourselves
another. You jig and amble, and you lisp . . . [III, i]

You could say this today about women. They paint themselves, they jig and amble, are sex capitalists, have flogged their wiggling hips across the screens for the last half-century, pout, act coy and pursue sexual desirability in ten thousand different ways. This is not jaundiced male chauvinism but a fairly representational picture of male attitudes that have been hardened by the commercial sex-ploitation of women. So Shakespeare appears to have little time for women, and manages to crush most of his prejudices into his portrayal of two pathetic examples – Gertrude and Ophelia. Between them they seem to share half the faults of man- or rather womankind, from Ophelia's treachery and naïvety to the bin of filthy lust epitomized by Gertrude. So, *nor woman neither* is a little safety net to catch any stray thought that some curious member might have about Shakespeare's private life. Let us not forget that in Elizabethan society homosexuality was a grave sin that could be punished even by death.

We cut the rest of the commentary that follows. It is very interesting but holds us up in the area we wish to follow – which is the plot. So we are into:

Hamlet   **Gentlemen . . . you are welcome. But my uncle-**
         father and aunt-mother are deceived . . . I am but mad

north-north-west. When the wind is southerly, I know a hawk from a handsaw.

Tell you the truth, you can slave for days for a meaning but it doesn't matter a fart because we understand the implication. We need not sweat whether handsaw means Henshaw. The main point is that it has somehow got lost – perhaps in a typographical error, and we are left with a hawk, which is a bird of prey, and a handsaw, which cuts wood. Anyway, I left it at that because nobody would know what a Henshaw was anyway; and I put my finger in my mouth and let it out with a loud plop, the way kids do when they pull the mouth to one side when it is full of air and with the wet finger test the wind. *When the wind is southerly* – i.e., 'When it does not make me mad', for *I am but mad north-north-west*. If I felt like it I would continue by miming the sound of a saw – but I don't think this was a particularly interesting or brave bit of biz. It left Rosencrantz and Guildenstern bewildered and Hamlet 'mad'.

Polonius comes running on and we listen to his news with an upper-class lack of interest. We have heard it all. I have cut the remarks of superior twittery about Polonius since it seems to be out of character for Hamlet to be abusive to others; also – lest you think I have some moral muscle somewhere that needs flexing – I may add that the real reason is that all this capering is boring. So Auker comes racing on with his news and we sit stage right and listen to him – or rather, watch him; for he now performs one of the funniest moments of the play . . .

Polonius goes through the list and feels that he must act out the roles like an old ham actor. He wishes to amuse Hamlet with his wit and so he is not just saying these familiar lines but also giving a graphic description of them. It is a cabaret act. He leaps across the stage for *historical-pastoral*; stabs himself for the *tragedy*; a finger on his nose for *comedy*, and blows a raspberry for *pastoral*. And then he proceeds to mix them up at great speed. He is like a huge farm-horse lolling across the stage, or a great sweating schoolboy with his large porcine face. He works hard at this and very often gets a round of applause at the end. It is funny, outrageous and daring. The audience laughs, and the players enter . . . THE ACTORS.

During this scene I had some very strange thoughts. At the end of Polonius's scene David Auker was so obsessed with getting it right that he would throw me a look that expressed in miniature how he felt the scene had gone. It was difficult and a bitch to do, although I have made it sound as if it was easy. Suddenly a man is taking the stage by himself, not just to talk but to lay his guts on the table in a piece of bravura acting. It is difficult and he makes it very natural. It is easy when you get on to the stage since there you either die or live but you can get off. And the audience are mostly middle class – and that is not merely an economic observation but a recognition that we – or not I personally but the Shakespeare purveyors and theatre purveyors – have driven any other class away from the theatre.

The audiences are receptive and a bit sleepy – a bit docile and easily pleased; not very demanding because if they were, what would they be doing there anyway? I know nobody of any real discrimination who goes to the theatre. No one. No one who would consciously go and see Shakespeare as minced out today. But I do see a lot of really pleasant, nice decent folks in the foyer, gallantly and gently queuing for their coffee, who are really satisfied with anything.

When I saw one of our great actors make a mess of Hamlet under the messiest production of all time at a major theatre, I knew in my heart that Hamlet had been betrayed, as had Shakespeare. We can't always create masterpieces, and the best actors and directors can go astray. But this once-great actor was sending people to sleep in droves – or the show was. Who protested? Our little gaggle of people sat and watched the play. We all know the story and many people are familiar with the text. Going to the theatre merely for the novelty of seeing and hearing a different voice is not enough. You may as well get up and do the speeches yourself. There should be some reason to see the play again and again. It is not an opera where we may indeed be content to hear just another singer; it is a play that is a living mirror for whatever period we live in. And just as the actor can make Hamlet express the thoughts of a twentieth-century man, so the theatre and the director should reflect our century.

Yes, Polonius had the audience on their toes, and I was comparing his attack on the part and his inventiveness to an act of bravery. Well, so it was, and very funny, and it made the audience rethink the whole part, and it made them look at that bit afresh, and it stimulated the ones who had seen it.

The players.
  On the line,
    Polonius . . . **these are the only men.**
the actors or visiting players fly on to the stage. We devised a travelling troupe of acrobats and street performers. In a ballet class I once saw a teacher demonstrate a leap by using his hands to mime the action, and the class was able to see quite clearly what the teacher had in mind. His hands seemed to symbolize the body of the dancer as it leaped through the air, and for a jeté his hands would flutter up and down. So each of the players came on and pretended to execute a series of dizzying somersaults and backflips by running on the spot as if they were actually going to leap, and then finishing the gesture with their hands circling the air – as if to indicate the number of times they did it – and at the end jumping into the last position: as in a film where the camera would catch the first moment when the actor pretended the stunt before the stuntman took over and the actor would come in at the end where he would be filmed falling into place. They all performed stunts. One swallowed a large knife, and another walked a tightrope at a perilous height, while another did a juggling act with countless balls. It was very funny for the audience who saw the joke, and they clapped each one in turn – the drummer giving, of course, a drum roll before each 'turn'.

After this they proceeded to line up to be inspected by the 'Royal Family', in the style of the Royal Command Performance. At this point I begin the lines . . .
    Hamlet **You are welcome masters. Welcome all.**
Mother, Ophelia and I walk down the line, mimicking the indulgent

and waxen faces of a privileged society being oily to the working actors, and hamming in dumb show the mannerisms and gestures of the *noblesse*. The shaking of the shoulders as a joke is shared between the peons and the prince, the arch mouthing, the tight grimaces. It was all very good fun and not out of character for a modern-dress performance of *Hamlet*.

I then beg for a speech:

> *Hamlet*   **Come, give us a taste of your quality. Come, a passionate speech.**

We have cut the rest of the speech which smacks very heavily of patronage and is also very indulgent for a man who doesn't wish to be thought pedantic or academic. His preface, before he actually gets to the speech he *chiefly loved*, is full of opinionated banter. So, anyway, he gets to the point without the preface celebrating his good taste. I sit, and the actor begins the speech.

How we performed this (the first time) was by creating a mêlée at the beginning, running round and searching for props – i.e. a table – and setting it into position just in time for the actor doing the speech to leap upon it, Fairbanks-style, and begin. The other players would group around him, as if listening to a favourite of theirs. Then, when they left, I would try to impersonate the player by leaping on to the table and trying to reach the same emotional power and be moved in the same way as the player. I used certain parts of the speech for this – in particular from *Bloody, bawdy villain!* Then, in frustration, unable to achieve in real life the catharsis that the player had received in acting, I kicked the table over and wept in utter frustration. After the players left I felt alone and had a secret desire to be like one of them. So when I leaped on to the table it was a sign that I could accomplish my mission; but I could not even act it out.

The next time round Barry Philips, who was a very fine First Player, didn't join us, so David Meyer became the First Player. While he was excellent as Rosencrantz, he failed to get quite the heroic drive that Philips had and which unleashed so powerful a response in me. He was a serpentine, oily Rosencrantz, but these qualities are not needed for the First Player who must inspire both

Hamlet and the audience. So, during rehearsals and viewing, the problem would arise.

I was put in mind of a theatrical group in the late-sixties experimental style, or even of my own group in the early seventies when movement was a new-found liberation for us, contrasting as it did with the inflexibly rigid spine of conventional theatre.

I HAVE NEVER REALLY GIVEN UP THE CONCEPT, EITHER, THAT THE PLAY SHOULD MOVE PHYSICALLY AND DYNAMICALLY, BUT I AM PERHAPS LESS FANATICAL ABOUT IT NOW AND DIDN'T PRECEDE EACH REHEARSAL WITH AN HOUR'S OBLIGATORY MOVEMENT WHICH WOULD HAVE EXHAUSTED BOTH ME AND THE CAST — ALTHOUGH I MUST ADMIT THAT THESE EXERCISES UNLOCKED MANY DOORS FOR US. NOW WE WOULD ACHIEVE THE SAME RESULTS BY IMPROVING AND IMPROVISING VARIOUS WAYS OF EXAMINING A SCENE AND LET THE UNCONSCIOUS FIND ITS OWN DIRECTION. I TOOK PERHAPS THE MOST DOCTRINAIRE IDEAS OF AN 'EXPERIMENTAL FRINGE GROUP' THAT RELIED HEAVILY UPON THE KIND OF MOVEMENT WE ARE TALKING ABOUT. FOR AN EXERCISE IN THE REHEARSAL WE WOULD TAKE A MOVEMENT OR SHAPE, AND PASS IT ON TO A NEIGHBOUR WHO WOULD OBSERVE AND KEENLY REPRODUCE THE MOVE AND THEN PASS IT ON TO HIS NEIGHBOUR — AND ALL THE ACTORS WOULD TRY TO RETAIN THE INTEGRITY OF THE ORIGINAL MOVE. THEN, AS WE BUILT UP CONFIDENCE IN IT, WE WOULD TRY IT FASTER AND FASTER UNTIL WE COULD ALMOST ANTICIPATE THE MOVE AND NOT WAIT FOR IT. SOMETIMES WE WOULD DO THIS WITH A GESTURE AND SOMETIMES WITH A SOUND AND SOMETIMES WITH A COMBINATION OF BOTH, OR EVEN WITH WORDS AND IDEAS. THEN WE WOULD CHANGE THE INFORMATION AS IT CAME TO US VERY SUBTLY BY ADDING ONE COMPONENT TO IT BEFORE SENDING THE GESTURE ON ITS WAY. OR ELSE A GROUP WOULD BE A MIRROR FOR A PROTAGONIST AND REFLECT, WHILE NOT MIMICKING, THE CHARACTER OF THE PROTAGONIST. AND IN THIS WAY THE CHORUS ACTED AS A CROWD,

IF YOU LIKE, RESPONDING IN THE WAY A GROUP OF PEOPLE WOULD TO AN ACCIDENT OR AN EVENT IN THE STREET. WHILE NOT IMITATING THE EVENT, THEIR GESTURES CREATE A CHORUS AND AN AMPLIFICATION OF IT: I.E. IF IN A FILM YOU SEE A GROUP OF PEOPLE WHOSE FACES REFLECT THE HORROR OF WHAT THEY HAVE JUST SEEN, ONE HARDLY NEEDS THE CAMERA TO FOCUS ON THE REAL SOURCE OF THEIR HORROR, SINCE THE CHORUS REACTION OF THE CROWD IS SUFFICIENT TO AROUSE OUR DEEPEST FEARS.

THIS TECHNIQUE ALSO SPARES US THE EMBARRASSING SIGHT OF A GROUP OF SPEAR-CARRIERS (NAME THE COMPANY OF YOUR CHOICE) WHO WOULD BE FORCED TO STAND AROUND AND PRETEND THEY ARE INVISIBLE WHILE THE HAMLET OR OTHER HERO MAKES HIS LONG SPEECH. THEY STAND THERE LIKE STATUES BECAUSE THE DIRECTOR DOESN'T KNOW WHAT TO DO WITH THEM. HE DOESN'T KNOW HOW TO (A) INVOLVE THEM, OR (B) MAKE THEM PART OF THE ACTION OR COMMENT ON THE SPEECH. THIS DOESN'T MEAN THAT YOU HAVE TO HAVE THEM TWINING ROUND THE ANKLES OF THE PROTAGONIST, BUT THINK WHAT YOU CAN DO WITH PEOPLE RATHER THAN PRETEND THEY ARE NOT THERE. BUT DEAD THEATRE SMACKS OF THIS. DIRECTORS THINK OF THEATRE MERELY AS LITERATURE THAT HAPPENS TO BE ON STAGE, AND NOT AS A MOVING LIFE FORCE. FOR THEM, THEATRE IS ALWAYS LITERATURE, AND DRAMA IS THE ELECTRICITY AN ACTOR MIGHT ACHIEVE INSIDE THE STRUCTURE. BUT THERE IS NO DRAMA INSIDE THE STRUCTURE ITSELF; IT IS SPOKEN LITERATURE, AND THE SUCCESS OF SPOKEN LITERATURE IS THAT IT CAN TRANSFER AWFULLY WELL TO THE RADIO OR TV WHEN THEATRE CAN BELONG ONLY TO THE LIVE STAGE. THE ACTOR SHOULD BE PART OF THE SCENE AND NOT BE WALLPAPER WHEN ANOTHER PLAYER IS SPEAKING. CAN YOU IMAGINE A STREET SCENE IN WHICH EVERYONE STANDS FROZEN WHEN THE PERSON DESCRIBES THE ACCIDENT TO THE POLICE? UNLESS THE ACTORS ARE OFF STAGE, IT IS POSSIBLE TO INVOLVE THEM ON ALL LEVELS WITH NO DETRIMENT TO THE PLAYER OR THE PLOT.

81

In this scene we decide to emulate the worst excesses of the period –
excesses that arose out of the liberating and intoxicating newness of it
all. So the actor made his speech to the accompaniment of some
strange backing – some reflective and some satirical. The players
were naturally all the actors, since we only had ten in the troupe.
They mimed the sequence as I have described, which was, as I say, a
slight camouflage for some indifferent acting, and also became a
comment on the acting style of the time. It was very funny, but
perhaps a mite difficult for me to follow. But . . . I left them on the
stage just as the First Player came to the end of his speech:

    First Player   **And passion in the gods.**

I shouted out, 'Oh!' as if they had triggered something off inside me. I
shouted it out and they froze, as if in the mind's eye. I must add that
the whole company was included in the scene – except the two
women – and the chorus acted out the storm, the *Striking too short at
Greeks*, and at *the mobbled queen* became her willing tears – in unison
of course. The effect was of an early experimental company visiting
Oxford, or some other university town, for a special performance.

   So, as I was saying, they had come to this point when Polonius
usually says *Look where he . . . has tears in's eyes*. But now, in our
second version, we axed it, and left the First Player frozen. Hamlet's
speech takes place in his mind and probably during the time the First
Player is on the stage. Convention demands that we take the players
off so that Hamlet can continue unimpeded; but the speech that I
make was of course inspired by the First Player and during the First
Player's acting. It might have all taken place in a series of quick
flashes as the First Player is leaving the stage. So we make a small
concession by leaving the players frozen for a split second while I
make the speech. (Of course, it is not a second but the time it takes to
make the speech.) During it, the First Player is always in my mind's
eye and the real eye of the audience who are being taken into my
mind.

    Hamlet   **O**

And the whole thing freezes.

           what a rogue and peasant slave am I!

Just sitting there watching the event as if a loony in the audience shouted out his mind; as if I can't believe what has gone on and what a complete idiot I am.

Is it not monstrous that this player here,
and of course here are the players on the stage to be part of my demonstration . . .

Tears in his eyes . . .
And so there were; and I take a small tear with the tip of my finger and show the audience the amazing phenomenon of a tear (mimed) in an unreal situation. I will use the players and make them part of the act – these players are naturally in my mind, as I have said.

What would he do
Had he the motive and the cue for passion
That I have?
Just what the hell would *he* do, since he could cry for a fiction what would he do for a fact?

He would drown the stage with tears,
Since this is a hyperbolic image, I can make it so. I see the First Player in front of me and try to impersonate him, the way years ago one would try to impersonate Olivier. I impersonate the First Player because I want to achieve his power. So *He would drown the stage with tears* had me trying to be the tragedian: the Olivier, Kean or Irving. A hammy performance, since Hamlet is not an actor but a ham. This is where we get the very expression: because Hamlet spends so much of his time wailing and moaning and cringing, he lends his name to overdoing something. So we are adding a critical dimension here by making this more of a lecture demonstration. I make my first attempt at grand passion and seriously overdo *tears in his eyes*. The audience – God forbid – must not think that it is *I* that am being hammy, so it must not be underdone. *Drown the stage with tears*, indeed – how preposterous. I stop acting and walk a pace or two, as if thinking of the next line – my dropping out should convince them that Hamlet is really an amateur who is trying to act like a tragedian. And it worked because the audience laughed and understood what I was trying to do, which may sound complex on the page but actually made things a

lot clearer by showing not only the face but, hopefully, the workings inside the face. It made the speech a lot less *vociferouus* and gave a critical insight into its mechanics.

And cleave the general ear [air] with horrid speech,

Shakespeare's metaphors are nothing but accurate. You cannot cleave or part an ear; you invade an ear but you cleave the air very easily. However, this is a point that could be taken either way. But, if you remember that he doesn't repeat within a line the same message, then it must be air since he mentions *eyes and ears* three lines later. He has mentioned all the things he would do, which is to *drown the stage* . . . *cleave the air* . . . *Make mad* . . . *appal* . . . *Confound* . . . *amaze* . . . *eyes and ears* – so you see there are no repetitions. So I *cleave the general air with horrid speech* – I cut a swathe through the air and stentorianly declaim again, because what I am doing is trying to get the fire of the First Player! I am trying ways until I find the formula that will set me going! *Make mad the guilty* – same thing, the impersonating of wild-eyed creature clutching his head; *appal the free* – same thing. The horror of such a thing; but by now I cannot make the thing work and so I must stop since I cannot use so many lines for this. The audience should by now have seen the dilemma . . . and so I stop 'acting' and take the last lines simply.

Yet I . . .

can say nothing . . .

I cannot set the world on fire with my performance, which is limp and weak compared to that of a great player.

peak

Like John-a-dreams

Saying nothing . . . no . . . not even for a king. The players are still there and still frozen in an attitude as if they were being caught like that in my mind as a memory that you bring back with one particular gesture. I look at them and ask them simply . . .

Am I a coward?

Am I? . . . Please tell me . . . Is that the truth of the situation? I ask the audience; I ask them, the players.

Who calls me villain, breaks my pate across,

Plucks off my beard and blows it in my face . . .

Nobody dare do that; nobody would have the gall. But it is just as if they did since they can do so much more – like murder my father and bed my mother. They may as well *tweak me by the nose* – life is already doing that to me and I do nothing. Nobody answers me and the players stand there, mute but watching. I take the lie into my lungs:

who does me this?

Who does me this!!! Of course, nobody except my own doubt.

Ha!

'Swounds, I should take it: for it cannot be
But I am pigeon-liver'd and lack gall
To make oppression bitter . . .

Here was a simple expression of a man confronting the truth of the situation – that he is pigeon-livered, not a hawk or an eagle but a soft little pigeon . . . a weak thing that lacks gall . . .

or ere this

So I make the change immediately on *or ere this*: I am renewed by the fact of the opposite, tickling and recharging my mind:

I should ha' fatted all the region kites
With this slave's offal.

Nice one: from one moment of self-scourging for being a pigeon to the next – the vision of Claudius wasted on some blasted hillside being ripped to shreds by birds of prey. Now this image feeds me more. Now, as I see Claudius in my mind's eye, I find him on the stage. The face of one of the players resembles Claudius, damn it! Yes, as I see him in front of me, the player that he is seems to turn into Claudius and I address the *Bloody, bawdy* section directly to him. He is there in my mind's eye and also in the audience's eye. I walk up to the figure:

Bloody, bawdy villain!

I then walk away. It could not be him. I turn suddenly, as if challenging my own perceptions. I stare at him. Is it?

Remorseless, treacherous, lecherous, kindless villain!

I turn on this Tussaud waxwork effigy. I spit the lines in his face. The figure does nothing but his eyes seem to follow me; a slight hint – but very slight – of a smile appears on his face.

O vengeance!

I shout out. It just stares back. I clench my fists; I want to punch him, hit him, smash his face, attack, tear him all to pieces. I see Claudius now without question since the actor playing Claudius is now doubling as a player. So this economy breeds some interesting metaphysical touches – after all, we are all players. Have you not seen this in film when a person obsessed with an idea of someone they love or hate seems to see them in every crowd? I see this bloated king's face in front of me and in my mind I take his body . . . I actually take my hands and make a movement as if I was taking him or his shadow and dragging him to the floor. I mime the figure beneath me as I pound away at space; I fantasize all the things I would like to do to him – and being purged of this glut of hatred, Hamlet is able to think straight and plan a clever strategy. Naturally, Shakespeare realized that the air has to be cleared by a huge purge to free one's mind: here is a classic example of Elizabethan therapy.

So I am on top of him and I see the filthy wretch beneath me: his smiling face. I pummel it until my fists bleed and (as if) my knuckles are torn, bruised and battered. I stop my hysterical outburst. There is no one there. The effigy is still standing there but it has turned its head – as if Claudius by some magic (since he is such a demon) could invade other bodies, spy. Nothing there but my own flailing body.

Of course, in the imaginative resources of film, Claudius would be in his room pondering his fate as he stares into the fireplace, while, at the same time, something may reach him across the thick yards of palace stone that may make him shudder for a second – this boiling hatred must send out something that wends its way to him. But here Claudius is the player on the stage. He is merely a player – as are we all – even if I choose not to think of him in that way. He becomes the King and slowly turns his head and watches the event, and then turns back. Did it move? Is it real?

I recover . . . and see my own stupidity, but only because I had an emotional and cathartic purge in my ritualistic, or symbolic, slaying of Claudius:

Why, what an ass am I!

I recover; I see the stupidity of it; I ask the audience's indulgence in witnessing this pathetic display. As if to say, 'My God, what happened to me?' I snap out of it on *Why, what an ass am I!* I can barely believe what I have just done; the audience react – they too have been here before and purged some taste for revenge in fantasy since it is safer to do this than actually to give vent to the murderous feelings that would cause actual damage. So in the purging one is freed. But here the purging merely wasted all the venom that would have been better spent on the King.

However, I can think now, and become aware of myself, now that I am out of the storm:

> **This is most brave,**
> **That I, the son of a dear father murder'd,**
> **Prompted to my revenge by heaven and hell,**
> **Must like a whore unpack my heart with words**
> **And fall a-cursing like a very drab,**
> **A scullion! Fie upon't! Foh!**
> **About, my brains.**

Yes, clarity and a bit of self-flagellation; a bit red-faced in the mirror witnessing the impotence of flailing around, but at the same time acknowledging the real therapeutic value of my fury, in that it cleared the air for some real good plans. *About, my brains* – I want to beat some sense into my brain, I want to cudgel myself for being stupid; I want to beat some sense into my head. I hit my head with my fists; I suddenly look up at the audience staring at me, following with respect and tolerance my demonstrations. They are so still, staring at me and just waiting for me to continue . . . wave upon wave of faces sitting still as ghosts . . . row upon row of eggs . . . this sea of bland expectant faces, sitting calmly there.

Then:

> **I have heard**
> **That guilty creatures sitting at a play . . .**

87

Yes; the idea comes here. I address the line to the audience. They are
the guilty creatures whose guilt will be touched by whatever crime
exists in the play that finds its reflection in them. *Our withers are
unwrung* [III, ii] – so, guilt is touched off by the spark that is struck
between pen and paper, and the audience's mind is like a dry powder
keg, ready to make a series of explosions. So much for identification.

> **Have, by the very cunning of the scene,**
> **Been struck so to the soul that presently**
> **They have proclaim'd their malefactions.**

By example; guilt through empathy. Claudius will reveal himself by
identification since we all reveal what moves us when we are watching
and involved.

So Hamlet invents the first lie-detector:

> **I'll have these players . . .**

(who are still conveniently on stage)

> **Play something like the murder of my father**
> **Before mine uncle.**

I am elated . . . I am inspired . . . what a *coup*! I can barely contain
my excitement, for out of this dung-heap of my self-pity and guilt has
grown this marvellous strategy:

> **I know my course.**

Naturally, after the first enthusiasm, there comes on the downward
swing the possibility of failure. Hamlet is so much on the pendulum
between ecstasy and suicide that it is inevitable, after a brave or
inspired idea, that he becomes all the more depressed by the
possibility of failure:

> **Out of my weakness and my melancholy . . .**

However, Shakespeare chose to cut this see-saw and end it on:

> **The play's the thing**
> **Wherein I'll catch the conscience of the King.**

To go out in triumph and no more doubts; to end in an Irvingesque
pose as, once more, I am inspired by an idea which lights up my
whole being. The play's the thing! The players are still there. I
slipped behind the player who had made the First Player's speech
and, when I had finished my last line, I took over his gesture. When

he had been 'frozen' on *passion in the gods*, he left himself in a slightly heroic gesture, and it was this actor's pose that I tried to emulate when I had made the last couplet. Watching and taking his pose I said:

> **The play's the thing**
> **Wherein I'll catch the conscience of the King.**

ACT III

SCENE I

The players now change from their secondary roles into their primary roles, leaving me frozen on stage since *I* am in *their* minds' eye and the position of the previous scene is reversed. Claudius is being trailed by the spore of the court – chiefly Rosencrantz and Guildenstern, Polonius, Ophelia – and Gertrude is also there, leading the small procession with the King.

Music plays, tense, nervous and jerky; and this is matched by the unevenness of the players' movement, which is watchful and bird-like, full of gestures that denote unease, paranoia – heads jerking round at some possible spy lurking in the corner. They scurry here and there like ants picking up bits of information and carrying it back to the King and Queen who remain the centre of attention. All the players move, and then stop in unison while one player discharges his previous cargo of information, and then the scurrying starts again. I believe we had two ways of doing this scene: one, as scurrying termites with information, assembling and reassembling, and the second time we did it we performed the scene slowly and sluggishly, following the King and Queen like the tracks from two fat silver snails. Rosencrantz and Guildenstern slink, bent-backed, carrying their slugs of news regarding the players; Polonius comes next, relaying his plan to send his daughter procuring for news, hence the fishmonger sending out the bait. He stage-manages a hammy scene to enable the King and himself to spy on Hamlet: Ophelia will walk in the lobby and come across Hamlet. Of course I have heard them because I am on the stage – thus symbolizing the fact that I am always there and they cannot hide anything from me. Nevertheless there is something eerie about being seen and talked about at the same time – as if I were invisible to them but visible to the audience.

They hear me coming and disappear behind the chairs as if they were behind the walls of the 'arras'.

To Be.

Hamlet **To be, or not to be,**

A hard walk downstage, stop and deliver the words as if I had said 'stand and deliver' . . . then lower my voice:

that is the question:

Sometimes I would find this a way of starting to get over the self-consciousness at the beginning of a purple passage, and so I was in it before the audience had noticed, and then I rested to let them take it in. Other times I might start in very slowly indeed, as a kind of confession of my problem, but always directly to them. If I started it hard and quickly then it would appear to be the apotheosis of many hours of thought – as if bursting through the skin of my thoughts it reveals itself: after all the *Angst* of indecision, life is condensed finally into *To be or not to be*. I stand and face the audience with the plight of my problem and my working out of it as a simple but difficult exegesis which my voicing can purge and perhaps answer. There are times in the play when Hamlet can drop the act, and this is one of them – when all character falls away and one is left merely with the man. To be simple . . . it is the only way; almost to drop any semblance of acting and therefore any trace of the emotion that the words might have for one. Now is the simple explanation of life, and one must say these words as if for the first time. These thoughts are minted fresh from my mind because I need help; they drop out . . . they fall away from me.

Sometimes it would resemble a dialogue with the audience, as if I was expecting an answer:

Whether 'tis nobler in the mind to suffer

(slight pause, as if in suffering this there is a kind of virtue)

The slings and arrows of outrageous fortune,

Or (*pause*) **to take arms**

Be purposeful . . . the opposite of suffering . . .

against a sea of troubles

And by opposing

(small pause as if to say, 'What would happen if we opposed them?')

end them.

Of course! What else would happen? If one takes action there is a result . . . but no action has no result and no solution . . .

To die,

Such a relief . . .

to sleep;

No more:

and then the explanation:

and by a sleep to say we end

The heart-ache and the thousand natural shocks

That flesh is heir to:

I confide, a trifle intimately:

Pensive pose as I contemplate the thin house.

'tis a consummation

Devoutly to be wish'd.

Wouldn't you know . . . don't we all feel like this at times?

To die,

Let's look at this one as another possible option. Look at the audience
. . . such peace . . . such emptiness . . . expiration of breath even in
the saying of it . . . dying while speaking it! To sleep . . . to sleep?
Another nagging thought will always threaten a peaceful one. In the
state of *Angst*, whichever way one goes there will always be an
alternative. Hamlet is full of alternatives since every act has its
opposite in order to define the act itself – so both are necessary to the
act. To live is bad, but to die could be worse. We would . . . dream!
And since we dream in sleep – and nightmares at that – then imagine
the eternity of nightmares that might arise from an endless sleep. We
have had a taste of real sleep which is like a little death, and been
plagued by terrible visions, so imagine never being able to turn the
bloody thing off. Hamlet argues out of the pain of perpetual *Angst*:

to sleep;

Almost a question,

To sleep, perchance to dream –

Now up a semitone . . . we have found it now:

ay, there's the rub:

There it is, boy . . . as if the game's up . . . what dreams may *come*
. . . what horrors may actually *arrive*!!

When we have shuffled off this mortal coil,

Looking at myself as a piece of already departing flesh and amazed at
the solidarity of it still:

Must give us pause –

Nothing; just say it:

there's the respect

That makes calamity of so long life.

A difficult one. Why must I endure this calamity of so long life? Why
should this be so? It means the sting of a long life when one has to
suffer . . . so what should be a great joy becomes repugnant, if
burdened with calamity . . . and so there's the respect we give

possible endless nightmares. And so the speech could be not about the fruitlessness of Hamlet's varied and exciting life, but about the fruitlessness of a dull, mundane existence that Hamlet has taken on in weariness, perhaps through indecision about the murder of Claudius.

For who would bear the whips and scorns of time,

I ask the audience, as if rhetorically . . . I search their faces, bland and innocent, for an answer and would be indeed shocked to get one. I searched their faces in The Hague, in Düsseldorf and in Paris, and the audiences were always the same – politely looking on as if secretly engaging in some rite in which they had been privileged to partake: the world's most famous speech and done in English. They knew that this was *the* one, and they would politely and attentively become very quiet and still, most keen to follow each word and each change of thought. There is a curse on famous speeches that makes what was simple and direct suddenly complex and mysterious – too riddled with hidden depths to be easily mined, and having secret codes to get to the bottom of it and that will result in revelation. So one has to be all the more simple and clear: direct and honest – that will create the grandest possible effect. (But this is not what I always did, as I shall show later.)

I hold a dialogue with the audience now. All the things we suffer:

Th'oppressor's wrong,

Totally meaningless now to imply the wrong done to us by oppressors, but it sounds like 'oppressor is wrong';

the proud man's contumely,

Perhaps if I believe in it enough the very tone will translate itself through my mood.

The pangs of dispriz'd love,

with a small pause before *love* while thinking of Ophelia's treachery;

the law's delay,

The insolence of office, and the spurns

That patient merit of th'unworthy takes,

The list of grievances for which we have to suffer, mostly, it would seem, at the hands of others; not illness or misfortune but done by the state . . . the law . . . people's arrogance. I must not be tempted to

97

skate over these things but say each one as if it was the thing I hate the most and that has affected me personally.

When he himself might his quietus make
With a bare bodkin?

Not really enough to kill myself over, any of these – not really. They are not deaths in war of nearest and dearest, or incurable illness. I see things really getting to Shakespeare when forming his company and trying to curry favour and at the same time be provocative – and so perhaps this was his hell. But, as in recognition of the workers, we have:

Who would fardels bear,
To grunt and sweat under a weary life,
But that the dread of something after death,
The undiscover'd country, from whose bourn
No traveller returns, puzzles the will,

I did this piece as if in the process of working it out, as I have said, for the first time and not as if I had spent months trying to find an original way of doing it. I moved slowly downstage and spoke the lines as if with *uncertainty* and it was this that tricked my brain into believing it and I actually found that I was thinking it out:

from whose bourn
No traveller returns,

A slightly jokey elongation on *returns* – as if . . . oh ho ho . . . watch out if you decide on that one . . . Hmmmn hmmmn!

And makes us rather bear the ills we have
Than fly to others that we know not of?

A slight pause after *rather* . . . as if to say, after all this why not slide back to the first position? – so much more comfortable to stay where we are and not risk what we do not know, i.e. 'Let's put up with it, old boy'; and the pause gives weight to the decision that was born of it . . . think . . . and . . . OK, let's do it! So I have worked it out with the audience as a kind of cabalistic text . . . taking it to pieces . . . *after death* . . . the idea dawning, *The undiscover'd country* . . . look around . . . *from whose bourn / No traveller returns*. Signpost each word – like a warning. I wait for an affirmation – and so I say it for them:

>   **puzzles the will,**

I.e. makes us think again; doesn't really puzzle us so much as make us wonder. I took another look at this and thought it out as:

>   **And makes us** (*small pause*) **rather bear those ills we have**

Sure, we can take it, not only take it but prefer it:

>   **Than fly to others**

(small pause to brace us for the unmentionable)

>   **that we know not of?**
>   **Thus conscience does make cowards of us all,**

It is a discovery that at the end we are leading to the culprit *conscience* – it is the inevitable pitfall of a man of conscience, the same old conscience that weighs our every action with grains of sand and one grain more or less determines our destiny. Almost a shaking of the head as if to say, 'If only we could escape from the rigours of our conscience that we use as a stick to beat ourselves with . . .' *does make cowards of us all* – he is speaking to everyone but really I am speaking to myself about myself and my own conscience; or perhaps my inability to strike, because the Wittenberg mind is always seeking alternatives.

>   **the devil hath power**
>   **T'assume a pleasing shape** [II, ii]

Hamlet says after plotting the play scene. Alternatives always look nice, grass is greener, etc.

If Hamlet were a Jew he would find it difficult to kill Hitler. As he was about to kill him his schizoid way of thinking would create alternatives and he might see Hitler as the devil, sent by God to propel the Jews into the Holy Land. He could justify anything by the use of conscience; but is it conscience in the sense of soul-searching, or is it philosophical analysis that seeks to render passion impotent from the inability to act? When one fears to act on an idea one tends to analyse it to death and hope that the fear will be submerged by good sense, or the act rejected by selective thinking, and one chooses the responses that will fit in with one's fear. Philosophy enables us to understand the motor of passion but in taking it to pieces the motor is unable to work. We know its form and content but it won't save us.

And thus the native hue of resolution
Is sicklied o'er with the pale cast of thought,

Ah ha . . . conscience is taking a beating, as I suspected. It is no longer plain, wholesome and necessary conscience. Now come words like *sicklied o'er* and *pale*. It really is a further comment on the previous lines. Hamlet likes to add layer upon layer in a need to cover the territory from side to side and top to bottom. So I say the line as if I can't get anything together. I start it as if with a will:

And thus the native hue of resolution

Then downhill:

Is sicklied o'er with the pale cast of thought,

Sometimes I would make a gesture parodying Rodin's *The Thinker* – a man permanently trapped in his thought – just for a two-second mocking glimpse; and then again another layer of the same material being woven:

And enterprises of great pitch and moment
With this regard their currents turn awry
And lose the name of action.

When we think too much we lose the favourable tide and wait until the next, when we will again be confronted by the decision, but we will always wait until tomorrow. This acts like the two lines before: we set up the positive and show the negative. To 'lose the name of action through reflection' implied a kind of impotence. The reflection is born out of fear of action and creates a species of wisdom, an understanding, but never a tasting of 'what if?' That is a thrilling supposition that cannot be entertained since you wish to know the results before you begin. Whereas the hero will go into action with even half the picture of what might happen and trust to his own wits when he comes out the other side. But the coward or thinker will not take on an action unless he is at least 90 per cent confident what the outcome will be. And so we *lose the name of action*. So, wretched and feeling most impotent since he still has not been able to make up his mind but has to have it made up for him by fate. Since he cannot seize fate then it must seize him. Now in his frustration he faces Ophelia and in no uncertain way commits her to a life of misery, servitude, condemnation and vilification; now he lets out the spleen that should be going on the murder. But that is what cowards do; they let out on others the sins they cannot purge in their own lives – and so we lose the name of

action

The final word, that word which comes out of the mouth reluctantly – *action* – the determination to culminate all the thoughts in a final crushing act. In this speech I have tried to involve the audience by working it out and showing myself doing it, not as a culmination of all my thoughts but showing how one leads to another by association, and 'discovering' it with them; or performing self-analysis before them and winding up with an answer which is my own self-revelation. Too much analysis, like too much choke, can make you stall.

Other Ways of 'To Be' . . .

Of course there are a thousand ways to do this speech, but in the end you have to show the audience who you are. But before you reach that revelation you wish to astound by finding a completely 'new way'. I started *To be* . . . with a thousand different thoughts in mind, and all of them structured by a 'form' that would astound the audience – or so I thought. They were far from the truth but all contained aspects of it. If the speech had just been written as a universal monologue of self-doubt there would be no question but that it must be acted from within, and simply. But now this speech is a challenge and even a threat to one's inventive powers. You've never seen a *To be* . . . like this before, so make way!

I

With John Prior, our pianist and musician, I tried it as a man walking slowly around the perimeter of the stage, which was a square, since we played it originally in the round. I took the four corridors at right-angles as if walking down a corridor talking to myself. (This would have been ideal as a film with the camera tracking in front of me.)

I sweat in anticipation, wondering how I shall do it, and am still experimenting well into the tour – the unfinished piece of the jigsaw puzzle to complete. No other speech in the play seems to make this demand on me. So one day John was playing some chords on the piano and I started to envisage another way. Music often helps me to unlock some problem and I will even act to music. I walked the square with his chords taking up the mood, and as my mood intensified with the inner conflict he would take it up, and then I would speed up and attack the speech as a cry of pain, and what was reflective became a howl of anguish since the speech repeats its theme over and over, twisting backwards and forwards and pacing faster . . .

     Th'oppressor's wrong,

speeding up:

              the proud man's contumely,

faster and even faster:

      dispriz'd love . . .

      the law's delay . . .

      The insolence of office . . .

      the spurns . . .

      With a bare bodkin . . .

Climax – and then start again, pacing slowly:

             Who would fardels bear . . .

and start the whole process over again, reaching hysteria, in

     Thus conscience does make cowards of us all,

as if this final revelation brought about my catharsis. It was very exciting to do it like this. I tried it again and it worked. It brought an emotional release and the effect was extraordinary. I consulted the other actors and some liked it very much, and some thought it to be over the top – and hurt the whole.

Working as a director/actor you direct yourself, and I cannot say I suffered from this. You learn how to test the atmosphere and your colleagues, who by their silence or lack of it will be a gauge to your pursuance of the truth. But ultimately the test is your own and I cannot say I have lost on this account. In fact, I think I have been braver and far more daring in acting and staging than if I had had to wait for Joe Bloggs to direct me. Eventually you develop a third eye, which may be strengthened by standing on your own feet, and I think a lot more actors should try it. However, in this particular instance my motives were wrong: they were to challenge the speech with a bold and original interpretation that bore no relation to what had preceded it. Let alone what followed. I was seduced into trying to make memorable something that requires the greatest simplicity in the world to do, and that is to be – yourself.

So, during the run, I felt the speech followed too closely on *O what a rogue* . . . [II, ii], which was itself a passionate declaration of my loathing for the King. After that, how could I cope with *Get thee to a nunnery*? And so I dropped the pacing tiger idea.

2

Oh, and then I had a simply marvellous idea which was sensationally original and could be done quietly: I had been trying desperately to find a confessional way of doing this by walking now slowly downstage and back and taking the audience with me, pausing from time to time as if the words themselves punctuated my movement: walking, and then stopping on *perchance to dream – ay, there's the rub*; continue walking – very useful and brought the audience into your feelings. But even this wasn't satisfying, especially as we had to adapt the style in some theatres which had proscenium arches. And so the problem continued.

At one rehearsal, where we were no longer playing in the round and preparing for our first trip to Israel, I came across the idea of using a cut-throat razor held just above my wrist. Appalling as this may sound now, by its very novelty it seemed to work. Matthew Scurfield (Claudius) said, 'That's the most truthful you've done it.' On reflection I realize it might have been because I was so intent on making it work for my colleagues and concentrating so much on the text that what he probably saw was a great concentration of honesty, and the razor was a way for me to get into it, since I had not enough confidence in myself to play it without anything, and I mistakenly thought the razor would give me something 'different', something original and exciting – and 'How daring!' they would think. So I did it in Israel and there was a great hush from the audience for the beginning as I took a chair from the chorus line and calmly sat down and took the cut-throat out of my pocket and opened it . . . all done very slowly and deliberately . . . held it above my wrist as if I was to bring it slashing down and looked as if I might . . . waited and deliberated and then said *To be, or,* looked at the razor again, *not to be.* (I thought I had indeed taken the audience with me and I had probably shocked them into some kind of expectation and curious attention.) But after *Who would fardels bear,* the razor seemed to hang about like a spare euphemism on a honeymoon and I could find no real use for it. But I persevered a few more nights, and the audience with me.

3

Oh, I was clever this time when I went to the Round House, for that was in the round, and I did the speech turning slowly in the centre almost like a lighthouse, taking in the audience with my stare and going quickly past the empty seats which were like great slices of cake in that building and had been made bare by the worst reviews of my life. However, in Europe when we came to perform it, we had the best reviews of all time, so either I had improved it or there is more than a cultural difference between the nations. I had given up the pacing and the racing and the slow walk, and so I felt I must still astound them with something. I must still bring something they had never seen to this most famous and jaded of speeches.

I had worked, as I said, with Christopher Plummer, who in turn had worked with Tyrone Guthrie, and remembered how off the wall some of the inventions were. Invention is important to an actor if he can bring it off because it suggests that his mind is volatile and capable of taking the most bizarre reading of the text and still not only making it make sense, but actually by the wit of the actor illuminating something of the text. So that the actor really becomes a collaborator with the author – no longer merely an interpreter but a creator, and the audience will applaud him for his daring. Usually this means that an actor will be more brave than he is intelligent; but a combination of both – *then* you have great theatre.

Anyway, this time I came on and would not trust myself merely to say the speech, oh no! I imagined this speech to be as a lecture of Shakespeare – a lecture on life and not really related to the play but almost an interval, a summation of his ideas. And so I started, very bravely I thought, with drawing *To be, or not to be* in the air – as if it were on a blackboard. Yes, I blush to say I actually did it. So I would, like a professor delivering a lecture, approach the students and write on the board: *To be . . . or not . . . to be*; then, facing them, say, *that is the question*. Of course, by this time this did not go down so well with the company; but again, it was a terrific audience-grabber . . . *That* is the question of today's discussion, and then continue. Some actors several years later reminded me of this effect, and actually missed it when they came to see it a second time after I had removed it, and in spite of the reviews many people did want to see it again – including Dustin Hoffman, who came back with some colleagues the second time.

So this was the time I wrote on the imaginary board. Enough said about that.

In the end I had to come to the simple conclusion that one can be inventive and clear without any props and aids, and just as I had eschewed the use of sets as being the barren space in the mind of the director who needs to force realism on us, I had to do the same thing with my own speeches. I did it simply, and came straight forward and tried to deliver it like an arrow in the hearts of the spectators and think it out.

One day I was playing it in The Hague in a vast modern building, and Jan de Bleik, one of the old school of European producers who had taken all the great British tours around Europe, including the best of the RSC and the National Theatre, came up to me after one performance and said that my *To be* was the best he had ever heard; and knowing how many dozens he must have heard I was truly grateful and thought at last I had found the way. The tour was in 1982, three years after the original production. I kept a journal from which I am typing now, and at the time I wrote that, 'I thrust the first line like a spear into the audience and, once impaled, I climbed into their minds like a rock climber who, having made the first hook, uses that to grip on to and slowly inch the way up.'

Nunnery scene.

Not an easy scene either; and subject to endless rehearsals to make it fresh and for Hamlet not to come across like a petulant, whining, raging bastard who at last has a target that stands still and takes it. Again, I experimented endlessly and knowing that the King and Queen (in our production), and in fact the whole court, were watching led me to play it as if I knew for certain they were, and thus played it like one of those loonies you see shouting in the street. Again, I tried this in rehearsal and it worked a treat. Suddenly breaking up:

> *Hamlet* **Are you honest?**

Starting to increase the volume, but really breaking out on:

> **Get thee to a nunnery.**

and the continuing speech:

> **I am very proud . . .**

But again, like the razor idea, the raving shouter worked superbly for a short time but then had diminishing returns. Oh, how I laboured and agonized over that scene. Oh why did it cause me the greatest of agonies? I'd find it with Ophelia suddenly in a moment of inspiration, and then I'd beg her to do it again so that I could see where it had happened, and then I couldn't find the bloody thing; and then I'd make the poor girl go through it again to see where it went wrong; and on and on until both of us were totally exhausted. And the real reason why I couldn't get it was that it's a fakey scene. It posits the male 'enlightened' view about generalized womanhood and creates the heroic broken-hearted Hamlet shattered by Ophelia's deception and adding for my part an unconscious, misogynist and possibly homosexual denunciation of womanhood. So I thought it was fakey and I could bring it to life only when I didn't cast a pretty, sweet and sensitive Ophelia, but a real Ophelia who had hardly acted in her life; she was already a highly strung lady, living under immense pressure, for whom the added strain merely cracked an already brittle vessel:

Hamlet   **Nymph, in thy orisons**
    Be all my sins remember'd.

A little polite chat to start the action. Still everybody is watching from behind the chairs and sometimes I would be more conscious of boring the actors who were there every night than I would of boring the audience. But still, they are the chorus and by their expression and bodies are reinforcing the theme to the audience. I imagine them struggling to peek through the keyhole, jostling and struggling to get an eyeful of the action; admonishing each other with 'Sshh!' as they clamber to see.

Ophelia looks uncomfortable and sweaty. She's a stinking fish and not good bait. She unctuously and uncharacteristically asks:

Ophelia   **How does your honour for this many a day?**
I answer as formally:

Hamlet   **. . . well . . . well**
and then, as if I cannot think of another way of saying it, I add a third:
             . . . well.

after a long pause. Then she adds that she has some *remembrances* that she wants to return, but for what reason I could never be sure, since I have given her no reason or cause so far as I know to doubt my feelings for her. However, knowing that the bastards are listening, I perversely decide to throw some light on her own mental state:

Hamlet   **No, not I,**
    I never gave you aught.

Ophelia looks uncomfortable again and seeks to confirm for those listening ears her own credibility:

Ophelia   **My honour'd lord, you know right well you did,**
– as if to confirm for herself and confound any doubts. And adding some more evidence for the jury:

    And with them words of so sweet breath compos'd
    As made the things more rich.

She offers my trinkets back to me and I throw them away, so confirming that they meant nothing to me. I then ask her a small riddle that impugns her beauty, suggesting that it is used to compromise her honesty and that she has blatantly been whored out. It went over her head, and I think it went over most of the audience's heads too. So in the end I cut it out and went straight to:

Hamlet **I did love you once.**

I hold her for a moment and she seems very fragile and very beautiful. I love her again, and yet at the same time I can't stand her any more – I can't stand that female utter stupidity. I love her as a child – I love her intense sensibility and passion. But now the time is out of joint and we must live in the real world, and that is a place she is most unsuited to. She is too precious for this world.

I take her in my arms, not failing to notice the beads of accomplice's sweat on her brow. I feel her heart pounding like a sparrow fluttering against my breast . . . *I did love you once* . . . I am reminded of all the things I loved about her . . .

Ophelia **Indeed, my lord, you made me believe so.**

What is she saying? I forgot the bastards were listening for a moment, so carried away was I by her pathetic vulnerability until I heard those lines of her well aware of the others' ears . . . 'You *made* me believe . . .' Made!!! She hasn't the guts to say, 'I loved you too'! . . . No, again she has to be the stinking fish:

Hamlet **You should not have believed me . . . I loved you not.**

See how they swallow and choke on that one. But I say it suddenly as if mocking the earnestness of the prior statements – off-hand and lethal and thereby indicating that my first declaration was a wicked joke. I had to do that to wipe away my own vulnerability with the smokescreen of caddish behaviour. The suddenness of it in contrast with my first line invites a laugh from the audience – as if they are enjoying the game with me. An audience must identify with the protagonist even in his most evil flights since, in order to achieve empathy, they must suspend not only belief but all moral scruples as well, this being the pleasure of theatre-going: we are able to whore out our scruples and vicariously enjoy villainy.

Ophelia **I was the more deceived.**

She adds, being all the more deceived even now. Stupid woman – too stupid to see the machinations of the world, living in her wishful fantasy of hero worship, which we shall see in her description of an Arthurian knight: *The glass of fashion and the mould of form.* Since she cannot see the camouflage she is indeed too simple for our world.

>*Hamlet*   **Get thee to a nunnery. Why, wouldst thou be a**
>   **breeder of sinners?**

I do this very still, with my arm and finger pointing to an imaginary place. I don't know why this liberation of one limb can sometimes help an actor. Of course, I don't necessarily know the exact location of the nunnery, but pointing off stage seems to indicate that I do, or at least that she should go. Somewhere. In other words, 'Go. Get out. Away from me.' I become as still as death, just holding the scene in the aspic of my venom. Quiet and stalking her . . . let it out slowly . . . feeling the adrenalin starting to sluice through my stomach:

>*Hamlet*   **I am myself indifferent honest, but yet I could accuse**
>   **me of such things that it were better my mother had**
>   **not borne me.**

Now I pour into the hungry ears all the things they want to hear:

>   **I am very proud, revengeful, ambitious,**

(I now pose as the jealous prince, ousted from the throne by the usurping uncle.)

>   **with more**
>   **offences at my beck, than I have thoughts to put them in.**

I am advancing on her . . . trying to scare the poor thing to death. But what the hell is she doing? She is giggling – so unaccustomed to my act or new self that she thinks I am making a joke. Blast her. I'll show her that I mean it:

>   **We are arrant knaves . . .**

Pause here and add for good measure, sweeping a few more into my pan:

>   **all . . . Go thy ways to a nunnery.**

She makes to go but I have her cross downstage in front of me and demand:

>   **Where's your father?**

Ah, she falters, poor thing. She stumbles and even looks to the concealed place:

Ophelia **At home, my lord.**

She barely squeaks out . . . and then I roar:

Hamlet **Let the doors be shut upon him, that he may play
the fool nowhere but in's own house.**

I storm out . . . and hear her utter pitifully:

Ophelia **O help him, you sweet heavens.**

This incenses me, even if I have reddened their ears with my knowledge of their spying.

Now they know, I exult. I have told them that I am without question on to her. I bear down on her again:

Hamlet **If thou dost marry, I'll give thee this plague for
thy dowry: be thou as chaste as ice, as pure as snow . . .**

My body mocks the contortions of female modesty; I burlesque prudery and narcissism.

Get thee to a nunnery, farewell.

I make to go off again, and again I use this ruse to suggest to the watchers a fragmented mind that pirouettes like a crazy moth around a flame. I come back again, refreshed by a new thought, like a firework you think has spluttered out, only to crackle into life once more:

Or if thou wilt needs marry . . .

Hitting *needs*, as if reducing even more the variety of reasons for which one would marry, and hitting the smell of lust in *needs*:

**marry a fool; for wise men know well enough what
monsters you make of them.**

Now it occurs to me to use the famous cuckold image of the two fingers to the forehead that lately has crept into our physical vocabulary – this awful 'in quotation marks' where two fingers of each hand create a gesture when wiggled of inverted commas. People are seen doing this all the time, implying for them some worldliness, as if reducing the importance of what they are saying, e.g. 'Yes . . . he "directed" the play', with the fingers indicating the actor's contempt for the director or direction. I saw this manifesting itself like a plague of these little worms held up by all sorts of people. And so – lo and behold – the cuckold could become . . . *what* . . . *'monsters'* . . . *you make of them*; in other words you make 'cuckolds' of them and not monsters.

 Ophelia **Heavenly powers, restore him.**

Poor Ophelia really is a feed for Hamlet (or even for Shakespeare's masochistic attitude) in this scene where she, as a whinging wall-flower, makes her feeble little peeps to enable the 'man' to rage. Anyway, this last little peep of hers really does get to me and I rush back as if I was going to strike her. She winces but I take her by the face as if to gain a better look, and pass comment:

 Hamlet **God hath given you one face and you make**
    yourselves another.

I mimic her whining ways, these petty ways of women who exploit the differences between the sexes and use male weakness to further their aims. I mime woman's lipstick-painting grimaces in the mirror; also it symbolizes her double face to me:

   You jig and amble, and you lisp, you nickname God's
   creatures, and make your wantonness your ignorance.

That's typical.

   . . . it hath made me mad.

The final crunch – that's enough. I have proved to the eavesdroppers that I am mad – *north-north-west*.

 But in my act I may have touched on some truths I knew not of: my contempt for women and their double-dealing as in Gertrude's adultery with my uncle and therefore her abuse of me, and Ophelia's treachery in being used as a piece of bait by the fishmonger. Now, something for the pair of them:

   I say we will have no more marriage. Those that are
   married already – all but one – shall live;

All but the present incumbent who happens to be listening and who will therefore benefit from this simple piece of prophecy:

   the rest shall keep as they are.

What do I mean? Of course they shall stay as they are if they are living. But no; Hamlet says the rest shall *keep* as they are, which suggests being kept in the dull regions of married life.

To a nunnery, go.

And I dissolve upstage – and fully onstage; as if I have left but remain as an image.

This scene worked best for me when I could whip myself up into a rage on the first *Get thee to a nunnery*, and do it as an angry, contempt-filled insult, which is perhaps the obvious way to do it. But it would somehow ignite me if I could fill it with 'Go on, get out of here, you precious little twerp, and wear your little ashen face somewhere else.' If I could feel *that* I could light the fire and slowly let it crackle; it doesn't mean I should necessarily shout it, since the line is already an insult and witty at that. It really felt sometimes like a loathsome slug was sliding out of my mouth, cold, remote and bilious.

Once 'alive' in a scene you can do no wrong, and every actor knows what I mean since too often we 'sit' upon a scene like judges handing down sentences upon the crimes we ourselves have committed, even judging ourselves in the middle of these alleged offences: 'Oh shit, that was bloody awful.' But at other times we do away with the judge, sentence and criminal, and just flow with the scene and are part of it. In these times we are inspired and can do no wrong. Nothing can shake us and disaster is even welcomed as a challenge. It is an effervescence when all your nerves seem to light up and you score the jackpot; the sluice gates are open and the adrenalin is flowing freely. It's almost like a state of grace.

In the first scene Sally Bentley wore glasses and this seemed to suit the idea of Ophelia as a short-sighted young woman who lived through romantic novels. She has a fair complexion and delicate opalescent skin. As a dancer she wastes no physical effort and cuts through the air as if she were sculpting it. I first met her at the Dance Centre in Floral Street where I attempted to give mime classes when not 'working'. I always felt a terrible guilt when unemployed which has propelled me on many occasions into situations I was not always comfortable in. I was always fascinated by the immense number of possibilities – not only of mime but in the relationship of movement and acting silently to drama. I would use these classes both to teach the basic principles of mime that I had been taught at the Le Coq School and to invent and improvise and search for new keys towards discovering ideas that would heighten theatre. I was extremely frustrated – as I still am – by what stood for theatre where I saw no concept or vision or interpretation beyond the usual, 'Let's move the traffic round the stage.'

Ophelia   **O, what a noble mind is here o'erthrown!**

I remain centre stage, frozen as if caught in the image of her mind's eye as she describes me. There is no real need to leave the stage since I wish the audience to have the two images of her plight and his isolation. She circles me as one might circle a statue and makes comments on it. The speech seemed to resonate more with Hamlet there, as if the audience is taken into Ophelia's mind. The speech is an 'awkward' soliloquy in my opinion, put there for a pretty indication of Ophelia's sweet gentleness. Also, why are the watchers waiting after Hamlet has gone? Why do they conveniently wait for Ophelia to finish her speech, and then enter? And so, watching Hamlet as she describes him gave, I thought, an extra dimension to the scene.

The actors come on and stand in a semicircle round her. I decided to use the whole court, watching and plotting and following Claudius around like a great rotting tail.

King   **Love? His affections do not that way tend . . .**

Ophelia goes to the King, who ignores her, and then goes from one figure to the other, desperately searching their faces for a vestige of sympathy. But they all totally ignore her and are grimly concerned for their own safety and peace of mind. Ophelia has 'performed' well for them and now she is of little consequence. It is a semicircle of oppression, plotting and debating the best course in view of what they have just heard since:

King   **. . . I do doubt the hatch and the disclose**
      Will be some danger . . .

In fact there was a hint of murder in Hamlet's last speech. The group starts to move off in a lumpen, snail-like crawl as Ophelia is firmly rejected by her father:

> *Polonius*   **How now, Ophelia?**
> **You need not tell us what Lord Hamlet said,**
> **We heard it all.**

Ophelia is relegated to dumbness.

The Queen is entreated to 'perform' next as a double-check. I am still on the stage, having turned into a convenient prop of their minds, since their talking about me in a sense keeps me alive and also suggests that I am less important to them than a cipher. Ophelia crawls out after them, no longer any use to anybody; not to her family and not to Hamlet. Gertrude and Ophelia return to their seats and the group suddenly turns back into our group of actors.

SCENE II

I spring out of my frozen state and address the 'players' who sit obediently at the feet of the director, as if after a rehearsal:

> *Hamlet*   **Speak the speech, I pray you, as I pronounced it to**
> **you . . .**

They are no longer Claudius and Polonius and plotters, but actors. They could be my actors being directed by me. They crouch down and I give my 'notes' to them all. To each one I give a special direction, as if each flaw belonged to a particular actor. I have never liked giving notes after a run-through while the actors gather like schoolchildren waiting for approval or criticism, which, though meant to be helpful, being given publicly is always felt to be personal. I would rather wait until the next rehearsal and approach them individually before it starts, or merely rehearse the bit that wasn't working. So here I am, giving each one his notes and making the advice to the players really individual hints.

Up to now, the actors have not left the stage once. They have not had to drop out of their roles offstage and then rush on to resume them later. Nor have they sat in green rooms chatting and smoking a fag offstage. They are part of the traffic of life and of the play, and their constant presence demands that they keep the power of their concentration alive. To leave the stage would be to reduce the energy of the stage. There is something very familiar when you have been sitting on stage and acting and being a presence for more than an hour. There is an attention and concentration demanded that focus the actors' energy towards the events and eventually relax them until the stage becomes like their living room. In normal situations, the actors would be off the stage for most of the play. We would not even get to know them and they would have to 'rev up' each time they appeared. I would see the actors come on and feel the green room being brought on with them; I can almost sense the tea and fags. But equally there is something quite magical about the stage where I have seen actors coming on covered with 'prop' snow, and fully believed they had materialized out of another world – but this is rare. Usually the actor, having dispensed their lines, like poor Ophelia, is no longer of any use and sits in his little room contemplating his life and awaiting his next call. Much boredom ensues and also a sense of the smallness of one's role. There is no exploitation of the actor's skills beyond the role written by the author. But here the actors continually recharge their energy on the stage, and their constant presence is a continual and ever-changing chorus reflecting the events.

So, as I clapped my hands, the actors following Claudius returned and became the players.

> **in the very torrent, tempest, and, as I may say,**
> **whirlwind of your passion, you must acquire**
> **and beget a temperance that may give it smoothness.**

I would give to Claudius (Matthew Scurfield).

> **Be not too tame neither . . .**

I would say to gentle Sally Bentley (Ophelia). I was not talking to Claudius or Ophelia; they had flown out of my mind and I do not think the audience made that confusion either. They understood and followed the changes of roles of these 'players'. They knew that they were ghosts that we could turn into flesh at a second's notice.

> **. . . o'erstep not the modesty of nature.**

had to be for David Auker's bizarre Polonius.

I continued in this vein, speaking the lines gently and persuasively, a little in the manner of the skilled amateur and getting polite laughs from the players for my 'jokes':

> **I had as lief the town-crier spoke my lines.**

Hah hah hah . . . very funny, my lord, or in that mood – being almost like a Prince Charles trying to break the ice with the workers.

I pause at the end and look at them approvingly and admiringly, and break the awkwardness with an abrupt:

> **Go make you ready.**

They go off, but not really off; just enough to erase the scene and commence another, by taking the chairs and reassembling them into a circle that will seat the 'audience' for the play scene. Halfway to their destination they are stopped by my saying:

> **What ho, Horatio!**

They freeze in their tracks, and the next scene commences.

The actors have become a frozen backdrop suggesting activity and the scene to come. This focuses the scene with Horatio and by the sudden contrast of their stopping and Horatio and my starting. Against this waxen backdrop of half-seated and half-posed actors, I embrace him:

> *Hamlet* **Horatio, thou are e'en as just a man**
> **As e'er my conversation cop'd withal.**
>
> *Horatio* **O my dear lord.**

I want to embrace him; I suddenly want to hold on to the only sanctuary I have in a world that seems to be in a conspiracy against me. Seeing Horatio has reaffirmed my belief in honesty and sincerity as epitomized by him. I grip him by the shoulders, this symbol of all I hold to be holy, as if in doing so I am struggling to hold on to the values I cherish before they disintegrate. I look him directly in the eye and woo him with this undiluted affection. Naturally the poor man is embarrassed by this sudden display of devotion. There are times when in stress one steps outside oneself and seems to view the world and its people as symbols of what they express and less as individuals, more like repositories for sets of beliefs and opinions. Horatio modestly refuses the compliment and, realizing I have perhaps overstepped the mark, I hasten to add:

Hamlet   **Nay, do not think I flatter.**

I am almost chiding; stern, dogmatic, hitting *flatter*. It is both an emotional plea and an intellectual embrace. But naturally the modest Horatio would hate to think of himself as a walking epitome of my value system. I want him to know how it is for me, want him to be the recipient of this embrace as at last I can breathe again in his company. *Nay, do not think I flatter* – I am for real, not like the others who are always fanning compliments at each other. I add, almost jokingly:

> **. . . let the candied tongue lick absurd pomp,**
> **And crook the pregnant hinges of the knee**
> **Where thrift may follow fawning.**

What a mass of metaphor and analogies; hardly a word wasted – pure beef and no fat. I make a small gesture of a money-feeling hand on *thrift* – the way people rub their thumb against their fingers signifying banknotes. We both smile at my little act. We are complicit.

> **Give me that man**
> **That is not passion's slave, and I will wear him**
> **In my heart's core . . .**

I cut directly to this, since this line seemed to contain everything that went before it. Somehow I want to tell him everything; that even though he stands for all I respect, I also love him. These lines seem to sum up what Shakespeare felt about indulgence and satiety and compromising, wheedling opportunists.

GARY WHELAN, WHO PLAYED HORATIO, WAS A HORATIO TO MY BERKOFF . . . HE USED TO LIVE IN MY OLD NEIGHBOURHOOD OF ISLINGTON – WHICH WE HAVE BOTH DESERTED THOUGH VOWING AT ONE TIME NEVER TO DO SO – AND I WOULD MEET HIM FROM TIME TO TIME IN 'ALFREDO'S CAFÉ'. THIS WAS A THOROUGHLY WORKING-CLASS CAFÉ AT THE CORNER OF ESSEX ROAD AND ST PETER STREET, WITH FORMICA-TOPPED TABLES SERVING YOUR EGGS AND CHIPS, AND THICK BROWN TEA. IT WAS MY LOCAL FOR A

FEW YEARS AND MY FAVOURITE MEAL WAS TOASTED LIVER AND TOMATO SANDWICHES. GARY USED IT AS WELL, BUT WE NEVER KNEW EACH OTHER BEFORE HE AUDITIONED TO UNDERSTUDY IN MY PLAY *EAST* . . . HE WAS AROUND FOR A COUPLE OF MONTHS BEFORE THE SLUGGISH AND OSTRICH-LIKE ATTITUDE OF THE BRITISH PEOPLE CLOSED IT. SINCE THEN WE HAVE REMAINED FRIENDS. HE IS A TALL, STRONG, AFFABLE LONDONER OF IRISH DESCENT, SLIM AND STURDY AND NOT DISINCLINED TO SETTLE DISAGREEMENTS IN THE OLD-FASHIONED WAY WITH JACKETS OFF. HE IS A MOST UNLIKELY HORATIO IN THE CONVENTIONAL SENSE, WHICH IS PROBABLY WHY HE WAS, IN MY OPINION, SO GOOD. HE WAS AN ALLY TO ME . . . A SUPPORTER. HE WAS ALSO TAKING, CURIOUSLY ENOUGH, A COURSE IN PHILOSOPHY! SO HE WAS CERTAINLY NOT A DRIPPY CLOSET-QUEEN HORATIO, SO OFTEN SEEN LOITERING ON THE STAGES OF OUR MAIN THEATRES. IN THE EARLY DAYS, BEFORE THE ROUND HOUSE DÉBÂCLE, HE WOULD COME AND DISCUSS MY SCENES WITH ME. JUST BEFORE THE FIRST NIGHT I HAD A KNOTTED FEELING THROUGH ME, AND COULD NOT SORT OUT MY OBJECTIVES IN A COUPLE OF SCENES. OUT OF WEAKNESS OR INSECURITY I COULDN'T GET THE OPHELIA SCENE TOGETHER AT ALL, AND THIS WAS THE NIGHT BEFORE THE OPENING AND I WAS IN A FAIR OLD STATE. I WAS STILL TIRED FROM HAVING TOURED *HAMLET* THROUGH ISRAEL AND WAS BESET WITH A HOST OF PERSONAL PROBLEMS. HE SAT WITH ME AND WE DISCUSSED THE SCENE, AND WHEN HE DESCRIBED IT VIVIDLY IN PUNGENT ISLINGTON PARAPHRASE I CERTAINLY UNDERSTOOD. I HAD NOT SEEN IT IN A MODERN SENSE, ALTHOUGH I HAD AUTOMATICALLY TRANSLATED THE OTHER SCENES IN MY MIND TO CONTEMPORARY RELEVANCE. WHY COULD I NOT . . . ? I REALIZED WHY . . . I FELT TOO OLD TO PLAY THE BROKEN-HEARTED HAMLET AND JILTED LOVER. IT EMBARRASSED ME . . . IT WAS TOO 'ROMANTIC'. THERE IS NO PART ONE REALLY CANNOT ACT, BUT THIS WAS ONE THAT FELT ALIEN TO ME, ALWAYS. THIS DID NOT OCCUR TO ME AT THE TIME BUT ONLY AS I AM WRITING THIS. ANYWAY, IN HIS GRAPHIC ACCOUNT AND HUMOROUS DESCRIP-

TIONS OF THE SCENE I FOUND THE MEANS TO UNLOCK IT FOR MYSELF AS WELL AS I COULD UNDER THE CIRCUMSTANCES. HE HELPED ME . . . HE WAS MY HORATIO AND NOT A SPONGE, AS SHAKESPEARE'S HORATIO IS. GARY MADE MORE OF HIM THAN THAT, AND WE BOTH WORKED ON IT AND FLESHED OUT A STRONG VIRILE HUMAN BEING, AND A SOLDIER–PHILOSOPHER. I ALWAYS HAD A GOOD TIME WITH HIM ON TOUR AND ON STAGE. HIS GREAT COCKNEY–IRISH HUMOUR WITH ITS GRAPHIC AND NO DOUBT GROSSLY EXAGGERATED DESCRIPTIONS OF PAST SEX AND VIOLENCE HAD ALL OF US IN A STATE OF AWED FASCINATION; AND HE CERTAINLY COULD SPIN 'EM. HE WAS AWKWARD AND GRACE-FUL BY TURNS AND HAD THE ABILITY TO RELEASE A STRONG TIDE OF PASSION. WE SAT IN THE KITCHEN IN ISLINGTON FOR HOURS AND TOOK THE SCENES TO PIECES AND — WITH THAT SENSE OF REALITY THAT CERTAIN PEOPLE HAVE WHO HAVE NOT BLOCKED THEIR WAY TO THEIR INTUITION BY EDUCATION OR CONDITION-ING — WE SORTED OUT MY PROBLEMS. SO I COULD SAY WITH ALL SINCERITY, *thou art e'en as just a man* . . . ETC., ETC., AND REALLY MEAN IT. *SOMETHING TOO MUCH OF THIS?*

Now back to the play. This confession to Horatio is the quiet before the storm, or the moment when the train has paused at some remote track of country and one is able to observe the glories of nature before being whisked on again. I have to stay now on the train of the momentum I have discovered and can afford fewer and fewer of these reflections.

    Hamlet **There is a play tonight before the King . . .**
Straight in and quick . . . recapture the pace:
        Observe my uncle.
I have driven this speech along, fired by my enthusiasm, and ram these facts home into the pliant and listening face of Horatio. (Some actors are such wonderful listeners that they actually seem to draw the words out of you, while others seem to be like cliff faces that send the echo of your own voice back to you. Gary was certainly one of the former.)

119

Claudius is still there. As we mentioned before, all the actors are frozen in time in their last positions, providing a tense backdrop to the scene. The King is sitting there in my mind's eye:

> **Give him heedful note;**
> **For I mine eyes will rivet to his face . . .**

I approach the seated Claudius and on the line *rivet to his face* I claw the air with my hands just in front of his face, as if I were grasping with a seeing hand every nuance of his expression.

> **And after we will both our judgments join**
> **In censure of his seeming.**

Quick now, and decisive:

> **They are coming to the play . . .**
> **Get you a place.**

On this the group comes to life and the picture moves once more as we see the 'guests' laughing and chatting merrily. They are assembled in a circle and make the noises that an audience makes before the curtain goes up.

The players' scene.

I have run on stage like a loony – as if making the last-minute preparations with an enforced gaiety. Claudius sees me and feeds me the line:

> *King* **How fares our cousin Hamlet?**

What else can he say? I come antically in . . . I shout the next word:

> *Hamlet* **Excellent**

like a madman. The guests freeze instantly – something very uncomfortable about being near a loony. And then I would calm down on:

> **. . . of the chameleon's dish. I eat the air, promise-**
> **crammed. You cannot feed capons so.**

Sometimes the shout was just my way of expressing my anger and hate to the King and I would compress all that in the word *excellent* as if it was a dagger I was hurling at his heart. I now skip like a naughty child around the group, being humoured by this one and that one. Now on Polonius; he twists round in his chair. I goad him . . . the usual banter; except that this Polonius is fat, as he *should* be in my opinion:

       . . . **to kill so capital a calf there.**

patting his more than ample guts. Now David Auker, playing Polonius, can extract a laugh out of a stone, and refuses to pay lip-service to these what I call 'feed lines' of Shakespeare to prop up the 'hero' Hamlet. In other words, some characters are developed less organically since they are 'straight men' for Hamlet's wit, and this reduces the characters' integrity. So Polonius's line was another 'feed' line for Hamlet to take the piss. Auker played the line for the laugh making me, Hamlet, wait for the audience to quieten down. He was a cunning sod and therefore was protecting his territory, which as an actor is vital. But he played:

    Polonius   **Brutus killed me.**

as an aside to Claudius. Why was it funny? Because he said it as an afterthought to Claudius as if he thought Claudius might be weak on history! But it was, and broke the audience up. How can Hamlet wait to say: *It was a brute part of him to kill so capital a calf there*? It should follow on like a rapier parry. But I couldn't jump in and risk losing the line in the gales of laughter.

Auker had already 'won' the audience to a comic Polonius, witty and servile by turns. I was in fact showing defeat. Should I say to the actor, 'You mustn't play this line for a laugh since it holds up the flow of the scene'? Another director would no doubt have insisted, since the line was played a little perversely. Just because Claudius was sitting next to him and they were such conspirators . . . but I know that if Ophelia was sitting next to him he would have played it as if telling a history lesson to a little girl. How did I deal with it? I waited until the audience became silent again then delivered the line with deadly intent. But I could not help but feel awkward at this tiny section; and yet I could not and would not dream of Auker 'feeding' me the line.

I circle the group, relieved to be away from Polonius and into the more 'pliant' areas:

    Queen   **Come hither, my dear Hamlet, sit by me.**

asks Gertrude. I often did things subliminally, and when I started to think about them or analyse them, I would lose them. Here was one of those times when I did something so instinctively that it's difficult to recapture in words. On *sit by me*, I would get to her chair as if to sit by her and then do one of those sudden turns like 'Ooops, I'm in the wrong place', turning almost on the spot as if she were rather too disgusting to be near:

Hamlet   **No, good mother, here's metal more attractive.**

Everyone froze in shock at the implication to Ophelia and the disrespect to the mother, thus killing two birds, etc. I dislike intensely fake staged disapproval – gasps of the spectators, etc. So we emphasized and almost choreographed the reactions as extra huge. An orchestration of mass disapproval:

Hamlet   **Lady, shall I lie in your lap?**

Shocked reaction. Chorus: *Aaaaah!!* (and freeze).

Ophelia   **No, my lord.**

Hamlet   **I mean, my head upon your lap.**

Chorus: *sigh of relief.*

Ophelia   **Ay, my lord.**

Hamlet   **Do you think I meant count–** [cunt]

Chorus: *Aaaaaah!* Expression of horror . . . I continue:

                                        –ry matters?

Chorus: *sigh of relief . . .* etc.

This went on during this repartee with the alternate sighs of relief and shock and was exceedingly funny. So, by orchestrating them, we absolved them from the necessity of fake 'rhubarbing' which was so familiar to me in rep.

Ophelia   **You are merry, my lord.**

Hamlet   **. . . What should a man do but be merry? For look**
                you how cheerfully my mother looks and my father died
                within's two hours.

I move into the centre of the circle. I shame them before everyone but make myself the madman by saying two hours instead of perhaps two months which would really have been insulting. Somehow the insult is veiled to show undue haste:

Ophelia **Nay, 'tis twice two months, my lord.**

I am shocked, and put my hand camply to my cheek as if to say, 'My, how time flies':

    Hamlet . . . **O heavens, die two months ago and not**
        forgotten yet!

I become a mincing queen who couldn't give a fart; a limp-wristed flick in the air. Why camp? There is something viciously accurate in homosexual sarcasm. It is the wit of the underdog and outsider that has developed a sharp defence mechanism. Somehow we impersonate a camp delivery if we wish to barb a comment. Fellow thesps will know exactly what I mean. For example: you feel an actor trod on your lines or upstaged you in some way . . . it's difficult to express your pain realistically without sounding somehow 'precious' . . . so you might say, 'We've got our mum out there tonight, have we then?' . . . 'Oooh, she's being very bold', etc., etc. . . . and this is said by straight heterosexual men. It is a way of coating the pill just as Hamlet uses the guise of madness – within which I use the guise of camp to say something quite vicious. I cut the rest of his speech. That was enough. Finish on:

        . . . **half a year.**

I gesture to Horatio, who makes the speech to introduce the players. We cut the text and kept and enlarged the mime. It's a dull text and weighs the play down even more. The point to be made is the revelation to the King.

The mime.

   Since we are all players, it must follow that we can enact any role. Therefore it would seem the most natural thing in the world that the King and Queen and Ghost *act out their own roles*! Normally, a group of players would come on and do this; but this way showed the act as it really happened – as if in the mind's eye. In a sense the King and Queen are enacting the players who are enacting them. They become the caricatures of themselves. They play their inner lives and not the ones they present to the court. It was a special piece of theatre since it pulled back the veil on what is usually seen, which is a squirming and uncomfortable King. We have seen this for several hundred years. We must see it with the eyes of people who are familiar with Freud and Jung and the *alter ego*.

Claudius leaps up on:

Hamlet   This is one Lucianus, nephew to the King.

He impersonates a strange leaping devil, pirouetting to John Prior's music. The idea for this came partly from a mime exercise in which the actor creates an image and then steps away from it, allowing the audience to carry it in their minds. So Claudius does precisely this. The 'play' actually begins with the old King (Ghost), and Gertrude walking in the garden. The music is lyrical and they design huge hearts on their breasts which they then offer each other. We see birds and butterflies sculpted out of the air, and eventually he sleeps. The Queen is portrayed as a slightly marionette-like figure. Then Matthew Scurfield, as the usurper, appears like Mephistopheles

A typical line-up of our Danish court with Rory Edwards sitting in his 'I'll have another pint, squire' position.

performing his grotesque arabesques, and begins the text:

Lucianus **Thoughts black . . .**

In a high-pitched falsetto. He mimes the poisoning of the King and runs off shrieking and returns to his chair. He adopts the position of one who has been a watcher. He has been watching 'himself'. The 'King' who has been poisoned meanwhile dies a painful, awful death, which goes quite beyond mime and is for real. The scene now becomes less comic and more frighteningly bizarre. The Queen returns, sees her dead husband in a state of rigor mortis and screams – silently. The sounds reach Lucianus who leaps back on and affects great remorse, but woos her vulgarly and frantically, humping her in full view. He then snatches the crown from the dead King's head and, taking Gertrude, parades her in the circle and retreats – whereon they both sit down. Lucianus is sweating profusely from the effort he has made and this also suits the watching Claudius who is sweating from

'guilt'. Horatio and I stare at the King. If I am a little proud of this invention, I am prouder of the actors doing it since this scene very often earned a round of applause in Europe, as opposed to England. I always liked watching it. I felt it had a power and a style that was emblematic of the company and they lifted it above the ordinary to the expression of a dream. Especially aided by Prior's witty musical accompaniment.

Claudius wipes his brow. The tableau is frozen in horror. Only the eyes of the King, Horatio and myself lock. The King calls for lights. The lights snap on. Damn Claudius, the filthy gloating bastard. He rises slowly like a drunk trying vainly to assert some degree of normality. I toy with him now like the proverbial cat pawing its prey. He calls for lights again. A blinding white light comes on and exposes everything with a bitingly clear eye. The cast rises; the chairs are broken up and replaced on the outer perimeter of the stage. Confusion mounts. I imagine lights coming on throughout the castle. Everyone is shouting for lights now. People are escaping. Actors create a corridor: a tight, narrow corridor through which they are streaming, arms outstretched, attempting to claw their way out. Claudius is going the other way; he goes against the tide which almost pushes him over. At last he squirms his way through and as he reaches freedom he sees me. Horatio is there. I throw myself into his arms and he swings me around.

> Hamlet   **I'll take the ghost's word for a thousand pound.**
> **Didst perceive?**

> **Upon the talk of the poisoning?**

We cut most of the singing and *perdie* and Horatio's limp sycophanting to Hamlet with lines like:

> Horatio   **You might have rhymed.**

We get straight to the matter. We know that Shakespeare was a superb technician and that Hamlet needs time to allow Rosencrantz and Guildenstern to see the King and get orders and come all the way back. So Hamlet fools around with Horatio making this banter. But it feels awkward and what it is – a time-filler.

Rosencrantz and Guildenstern come rushing in:

Guildenstern **Good my lord, vouchsafe me a word with you.**

Hamlet **Sir, a whole history.**

I start walking around the stage and they follow me. I avoid them . . . it becomes like a game:

Guildenstern **The King, sir –**

Hamlet **Ay, sir, what of him?**

Guildenstern **Is in his retirement marvellous distempered.**

Hamlet (*Acting drunk*) **With drink, sir?**

Hints of Claudius's boozy nature. I am acting the madman again – the 'clever madman' who makes a fool of everyone to the delight of the young people in the audience who love nothing better than to see the agents of authority being put down. I put my arms around their necks with enforced gaiety.

Hamlet **You are welcome.**

Horatio comes and joins us and we become this tight, ugly little group in which something unpleasant could break out any second. They feel trapped; I release my hold and listen to them. They spout their message and I pace up and down in impatience:

Hamlet **O wonderful son, that can so 'stonish a mother!**

The audience laughs as if thinking what more can a son do to astonish a mother who is so intimate with his workings. We cut out the reference to *I lack advancement* – this ploy of continually dropping red herrings is getting boring and was one of the reasons the play always bored me in productions by directors who wish to be purist and shove the five-hour version down your throat. In the sixteenth century the play was probably the equivalent of our novel and contained an immense amount of detail. It was a slower age and the audience wanted everything to be filled in. If they saw Hamlet in one scene they knew that he couldn't appear in the next scene if Ophelia is to come on and tell her father how strange he had been. In the meantime, some time had to elapse for the event to happen, and this gives birth to inordinately dull scenes like that between Polonius and Reynaldo.

Hamlet **O, the recorders. Let me see one.**

127

I ask, as casually as asking for a light:

Will you play upon this pipe?

Interrupting our charged conversation as if, like the madman, I had already forgotten it.

I do beseech you.

I become imploring, wheedling like a child who wants his sweets. The two of them are fastened together and Horatio, no doubt using his Islington background as a source of inspiration, creates a barrier so that the two are effectively sandwiched between us. Horatio has his large hands on their two shoulders in a gentle fashion that has a hint of something unpleasant.

It is as easy as lying.

I am very reasonable and fail to understand why they cannot play this pipe. I still implore as one who is bitterly disappointed at a friend not playing when I suspect that he can and won't oblige. Still the loony – which changes suddenly and dramatically as I let down the mask and become forthright and angry. This is one of the very few moments in the production where there was any element of violence. I took the recorder and thrust it in Guildenstern's mouth. I made him give head to the recorder if you like, and forced him to play. Either he opens his mouth and receives it to play or his rotten teeth get caved in. He struggles with it and, in his effort to relieve himself of this position, obliges with a few squeaky notes. Guildenstern is furious with this kind of 'torture' and spits out . . .

> *Guildenstern* **But these cannot I command to any utterance of harmony. I have not the skill.**

He has now become embarrassed and confused and a bit angry. They both now look what they are, and their meagre façade of gentility has been ripped off. They both look like frightened sweaty schoolboys who have been caught cheating or wanking in the loo. They know that they have done something wrong, have been found out; but they cannot conjecture what their punishment may be. I become totally quiet and reasonable.

> *Hamlet* **Why, look you now, how unworthy a thing you make of me. You would play upon me, you would seem**

to know my stops . . .

I circle them. They follow me with their eyes. I am calm still . . . but increasing the intensity and coming eyeball to eyeball:

> . . . **you would pluck out the heart of my mystery** . . .

Close in, intimate, friendly, but with an icy chill moving in. I am amazed by their audacity:

> . . . **you would sound me from my lowest note to the top of my compass; and there is much music, excellent voice, in this little organ, yet you cannot make it speak. 'Sblood** . . .

Suddenly full taurean bellow or leonine roar:

> . . . **do you think I am easier to be played on than a pipe?**

They shrink back at the promise of violence contained in that roar, but Horatio has them trapped from behind:

> **Call me what instrument you will, though you fret me, you cannot play upon me.**

I slam down hard on the last *me*, really furious and allowing the *me* to suggest all kinds of reprisals for their behaviour. The scene works well and is clear. I signal to Horatio who has them by the collars like a couple of wet rabbits and throws them out.

I return to Horatio and in spite of or because of my anger we both collapse into a heap of laughter over the absurdity of it all. I intended to scare them shitless, and got involved in my own 'act'. I got carried away – although with good cause – and seeing Horatio punctured my swollen spleen. I could never be that violent in a calculated way. My violence has to be triggered suddenly – from finding someone hiding in the closet, from working myself up in the *rogue and peasant slave* speech, which, although not sudden, works by a series of associations. The recorder scene is rather calculated. It springs from my sense of opportunity and is satirical – a metaphor neatly coming to hand. I work myself up into a state with Rosencrantz and Guildenstern but it is calculated and inflated and therefore I laugh with Horatio after the event as it has been a good act. My violence has to be sudden and before I have time for my reason to defuse the time bomb of my emotions. So I laugh with Horatio and shake his hand. We 'did it'. We are for the first time fighting back. We are putting a little poison back into the King's ear and he doesn't like it . . . too much. I am excited by the unfamiliar stream of adrenalin flowing through my blood, which prompts a new view of myself. I had reversed the downward plunge of mindless suffering and vindicated the Ghost's word. I had proved beyond any shadow of doubt the King's to blame. I am in the killer mood. I say farewell to Horatio.

    Hamlet   **'Tis now the very witching time of night,**
        When churchyards yawn and hell itself breathes out
        Contagion to this world.

I wind myself up like a coiled spring – and release it:

        Now could I drink hot blood,

I am alive in the acids of my own rage . . . I leap into the air and tear a long *blooooood* out of my lungs.

        And do such bitter business as the day
        Would quake to look on.

I could . . . but I don't . . . Let's postpone it a little and let it all out on Mum:

        Soft, now to my mother.

I have to go there to straighten her out since she would naturally have failed to understand the play. I must tell her what has transpired or it will look like an ambition-inspired killing by a thwarted, jealous and frustrated wimp. I am almost in pain with desire to twist my sword in Claudius – but not yet.

    A drum beats and I pace round the stage as if I were measuring the paces to my mother's closet where in fact I should be walking to. In the round it was as if I was pacing the outer corridors of the castle. I would follow the exact rectangle and sharply turn the corners. I am pacing furiously down the corridor:

        O heart, lose not thy nature. Let not ever
        The soul of Nero enter this firm bosom;

Still pacing:

        Let me be cruel, not unnatural.

Still building up the heart to a furious beat; still winding up the spring to unleash the most vicious venom. For without it I know I shall fail, and so I must keep it boiling; for if it cools down my rational mind will sneak in and anaesthetize my action, so I use words that will continually spice my acid bath.

I will speak daggers to her, but use none.

My tongue and soul in this be hypocrites:

I must somehow keep the heart boiling and the tongue cold and hard. I have to be two people. Difficult. The drum continues to measure out the heartbeat . . . my heartbeat; also time that is inexorably running out for Claudius:

never, my soul, consent.

I finish the walk and sit.

And watch the next scene.

SCENE III

Although I am sitting, the drumbeat continues for me. I am, if you like, 'offstage' . . . and only my actor's body waits. The next scene is broken up into two short staccato sections. Impressions of constant movement: messengers flying in with news, spies on the alert . . . the palace, one huge ear. The drum continues to beat out Hamlet's footsteps to his mother which also serves as the beat for the walking feet. The cast paces to the rhythm of the drum and then freezes. The snake pit has been awakened. Rosencrantz and Guildenstern approach the King. The attitudes are of a tableau. It comes suddenly to life:

    King   **I like him not . . .**

Claudius pushes Rosencrantz over and sends him flying across the stage. Claudius is drunk and clutching his bottle, which he drinks from. They feebly try to ingratiate themselves and he dismisses them:

    Rosencrantz   **Never alone**

   Did the King sigh, but with a general groan.

More toadying from Rosencrantz. Yet how true. His last speech was cut. It stopped the pace and flow of the action and the King in his present state could hardly be expected to hear the philosophy of power from Rosencrantz. Claudius is in a hurry:

> *King* **Arm you, I pray you, to this speedy voyage,**
> **For we will fetters put about this fear**
> **Which now goes too free-footed.**

> *Rosencrantz*   **We will haste us.**

They go. The cast moves again to the beat of the drum.

Hamlet is still walking round the castle on his way to Gertrude. The pulse still beats and the blood flows faster. Patterns are created and broken. Eventually everyone freezes. Polonius tries to comfort the King with some plan and dull info.

> *Polonius* . . . **he's going to his mother's closet.**
> **Behind the arras I'll convey myself** . . .

The King now is the worse for drink, but offers some to Polonius, who wisely decides to remove the bottle from him. The cast move once more to the beat to dissolve the scene. This time, on the last beat of the drum they sit and we reveal the King.

The drum continues softly. Claudius is alone in his anguish. I am now sitting, waiting and alert, while my spiritual body continues the march. The King goes through his:

> *King* **O, my offence is rank, it smells to heaven**. . .

I pass the King's chamber on the way to my mother's closet, and stop . . . he is praying. Having finished his soliloquy of guilt, he is on his knees with his back towards me. Like a beast ready for slaughter . . . perfect timing . . . no one about . . .

> *Hamlet* **Now might I do it pat, now a is a-praying.**
> **And now I'll do't.**
> (*Draws sword.*)
>   **And so a goes to heaven;**
> **And so am I reveng'd.**

The previous speech Matthew Scurfield (Claudius) had directed straight at the audience. It is a difficult beast of a speech and he did it as a low moan, like a man who knows that he is on the bottom rung of the ladder that descends into hell and is pleading his case, not wishing to take the last step. I step on to the stage through the door from the

As I imagine I have slashed him, Claudius imagines it too. Or does he?

133

corridor. I am amazed at the offering as if from heaven, his back to me as a sacrifice. I take out my sword and approach.

I raise my invisible (mimed) shaft of steel. My eyes search out the best place and I decide to slash him across the neck which I do and he jerks forward turning his face as he does so; and then I stab again and again. I plunge it deep within, as if he were a stuck pig. Blood spurts out of his gashes. The piano plays a majestic, powerful scherzo and I leap into the air and arabesque round the stage. Then, just as quickly, as in those movies that run backwards, I retrace my steps and the King recovers his praying position. I had played the scene in my *imagination* between the drawing of the sword and

That would be scann'd:

– which I said just at the end of my jubilant dance. I am now back in the original stance . . . my imagination did a swift recce of the future – saw the blood and rejoiced in the act, but couldn't do it in the physical world.

I leave him praying and explore my thoughts further. I had relished and played the act in my mind to test its value, and found joy but also doubt. So I am unable to do the act for fear of the consequences, not fear of the act itself. He is praying – therefore he is ready for heaven.

> **A villain kills my father, and for that**
> **I, his sole son, do this same villain send**
> **To heaven.**

Now I intend to justify my indecision on the grounds that a praying villain will go to heaven – an absurd hypothesis since it allows any villainy on earth so long as one shows a moment of regret after the event. What I see is Hamlet's capacity for analysis taken to absurd degrees. What do I care as long as Claudius is no longer on earth?

> **A took my father grossly, full of bread,**
> **With all his crimes broad blown, as flush as May;**

So the old King is forced to walk the night until his *foul crimes . . . are burnt and purg'd away*. Shall Hamlet, then, take Claudius

> **in the purging of his soul,**
> **When he is fit and season'd for his passage?**
> **No.**

134

I'll take him in an evil act; drunk or gaming; penetrate him even as he penetrates my mother – lovely Jacobean revenge.

> . . . **in th'incestuous pleasure of his bed** . . .

Oh yeah? Promises, promises. Then, ironically, Claudius confesses that he has been nowhere near true confession since:

> *King* **My words fly up, my thoughts remain below.**
> **Words without thoughts never to heaven go.**

An accurate summary of bad acting.

SCENE IV

The closet scene.

My spleen is rising. The beat continues. I pace along the rectangle to my mother: the climax of my intentions. Rosencrantz and Guildenstern dealt with; the play scene exposed the villain; I nearly killed the King. Now . . . to blast my mother:

> *Hamlet* **Now, mother, what's the matter?**

Supreme irony; imputing the wrong and distress to Mum having her hysteria again. I am wound up like a tight spring. I have charged along the corridors fed by the extra adrenalin that popped into my stomach for the stabbing of Claudius and has not been used but has festered there like a boil about to burst. I must lance it.

I approach the large door. Two actors move silently into position to be the door. I bang heavily at the door. John pounds the drum and I hit space. I grab the actors' hands and pull them outwards. I am breathing heavily and sweating. The drum pulse has stopped. I prop one leg against the other, as if leaning on a door post, just standing looking, hands on hips. I say, *Now, mother, what's the matter?* This used to get a laugh from the audience and sometimes brought the house down. It is a volte-face – I decided to reverse gear. I am 'calm' – for a moment.

> *Queen* **Hamlet, thou hast thy father much offended.**

My response is to thrust her crime in her face:

Hamlet **Mother, you have my father much offended.**

She is confused while guilt begins to flush through her system, and she says:

Queen **Why, how now, Hamlet?**

I mock her whiningly:

Hamlet   **What's the matter now?**

I'm still at the door position. She appeals to a son's love:

Queen **Have you forgot me?**

Hamlet   **No,**

I answer:

                                       by the rood, not so.

        You are the . . .

And here I pretend to struggle to remember:

            Queen,

I gleefully recall who she is. And then to clarify it I add slowly and painstakingly the next four words, as if dragging the vaults of memory:

              your husband's brother's wife,
        And, would it were not so, you are my mother.

The humour at the beginning of the scene is very useful as an antidote to the intensity of what follows. Something unconscious seeks to create humour, to scour the audience for a laugh at gallows humour. There is an imp of truth there, a mean little maggot that wishes to collapse the whole rotten edifice of seriousness and pomposity.

  She now threatens:

Queen **Nay, then I'll set those to you that can speak.**

Who are those she threatens me with? A gaoler? Guards? My stepfather? Who will she set on to me? How dare she! As she goes to the door I swing her round and the force of her own pace sends her flying across the stage. There is no bed on our stage and no chairs. The stage is our everything. Having crashed across the stage I add gently:

Hamlet **Come, come, and sit you down,**

– after she has crashed, the expert dissimulation by the able and tough Linda Marlowe had me fooled,

136

>   **you shall not budge,**
>   **You go not till I set you up a glass**
>   **Where you may see the inmost part of you.**

The violence of the fall, which slid her halfway across the stage, combines with my attitude to make her think the worst:

> *Queen* **What wilt thou do? Thou wilt not murder me?**
>   **Help, ho!**

My heart was beating the drum which I excitedly followed. I didn't know what I felt any more, but it was enough for her to scream for help: *Thou wilt not murder me?* I had to show that possibility in my eyes. I had no idea I had become such a monster, wallowing over her crushed figure. We were in an empty space: no bed, no chair to take some of the responsibility off our bodies. We were figures without a landscape to refer to – emotions moving through this limbo, with nothing to soften and absorb the energy. No bed or carpet to soften the blow; no bed to withdraw to and play the Oedipal Hamlet. So our agonies reverberated like sparks in a closed room, bounding off the walls; no conductor to drain them away – just our two bodies and the floor as a bed, or a floor, or what you will. Only the other actors waiting and watching as a dumb chorus, reflecting the energy back to the centre.

Gertrude screams. Polonius has been hiding in the 'arras' or cloth recess. As he hears the Queen's cry for help he calls out. I freeze. Polonius freezes too. I stop the Queen's richly lipsticked mouth with my hand as soon as I see that she is becoming hysterical. Holding her revolting mouth tightly . . .

> *Hamlet* **How now? A rat!**

I release my bloody-looking hand from her mouth, which now looks like it has been punched red. I hear the beat again – or is it my heart? I have here no equivocation – my pulse is up again even higher than when I fought against killing the King earlier. Is my fate giving me another chance? I still have not purged myself of venom and each new event finds objects for it. My mother helps; her filthy lipstick helps as I take my hand from her mouth. I draw my invisible sword out – it is

137

so much more visible than the real blunt weapons you see on every stage in the land. This is the blade of the imagination and it is razor sharp – this blade I will thrust between the ribs with all my might and the audience will see and 'feel' every inch as it slides in. We do not need to see the real blade. We need to see the effort as it is thrust in: the shoulders hunched and the elbows pulled back . . . then stab . . . hard and quick. So I draw my sword out and gesture to her to keep quiet, which she does, believing that her life hangs on it. The stage goes deathly quiet. I move to the back wall and walk steadily and slowly to the 'arras' where David Auker is trembling as Polonius. I am inches away from him but an invisible curtain separates us. I can't 'see' him. I stab through the 'arras' and withdraw the sword. No blood on it. I have hit nothing. I stab again, and again feel space. The silence is deafening. Rarely have I heard an audience this silent. Since I am involving them and their minds in the game, we all see Polonius, we all see the sword. We also see that Hamlet doesn't 'see' Polonius. And so, with all these convolutions, we have tied up the audience's mind in a tricky web.

I am tormenting whoever is in the 'arras' trying to be silent and still while the sword of fate leaps in like an angry tongue. Polonius is in profile against the invisible cloth and trembles like a leaf. I stab again, and again – space. The tension now needs releasing and the blood of Polonius soon gushes out. I hear a whimper and I thrust to where the sound is, not even looking where I am thrusting, but hearing, keeping my eyes ahead so as better to focus the ears. It has to be released or it will explode within me. This time the sword hits something . . . it does not come out so easily . . . it sticks in fat and muscle. I pull it out and hear something cry . . . whimper. I stab again, I have located the sound . . . and yet again. He is pinned to my sword. Sweet bliss.

Dead for a ducat, dead.

Polonius slumps to the floor. I still can't see him since he is behind the invisible curtain. I pull the sword out more slowly and there is 'blood' on it.

SOME YEARS AGO I HAD THE GREAT EXPERIENCE OF WATCHING A POLISH MIME THEATRE AT SADLER'S WELLS. THERE WAS A SCENE TAKEN FROM A JAPANESE FOLK TALE WHERE A FARMER WAS PROTECTING AN ESCAPED PRISONER WHO WAS HIDING BEHIND A FENCE. A FIERCE SOLDIER COMES IN TO THE FARMYARD AND DEMANDS FROM THE FARMER THE PRISONER WHOM HE HAS SEEN TAKE COVER THERE. THE FARMER PROTECTING THE PRISONER PROTESTS HIS IGNORANCE. THE SOLDIER SAYS THAT HIDING PRISONERS OF WAR BRINGS A MANDATORY DEATH SENTENCE. THE FARMER REMAINS STOIC AND REVEALS NOTHING. THE PRISONER WE CAN SEE HIDING BEHIND A REAL FENCE. THE SOLDIER APPROACHES THE FENCE THINKING HE HAS HEARD SOMETHING, AND STABS THE FENCE. THE SWORD GOES THROUGH THE FENCE AND UNLUCKILY THROUGH THE PRISONER. THE DYING MAN, NOT WISHING THE FARMER TO BE ARRESTED, HOLDS THE BLADE BETWEEN HIS FOREFINGER AND THUMB AS IT LEAVES HIS BODY SO AS TO WIPE TRACES OF THE BLOOD OFF. THE SOLDIER PULLS OUT THE BLADE AND SEES THAT IT IS CLEAN, DECIDES HE HAS MADE A MISTAKE, AND LEAVES. THIS WAS THE INSPIRATION FOR THE SCENE WITH POLONIUS BEHIND THE 'ARRAS'.

I am exalted. I have done it. I was able to fulfil the promise in the blood. I acted. I did it. I let it go. The bolt was drawn and the beast in the blood leapt out. Who cares where? I was proud that, for the first time, I had been able to act without filtering my intention. I was at last able 'to be'. And I didn't question that it could be anyone but the King. I was sure. I knew it had to be him. I had stopped thinking or I might have realized that the King would hardly have had time to finish praying and dash to Gertrude's room before me! A little thought might have saved Polonius's life, but I was not into thinking – I was into proving myself to be equal to the task; something I had lamentably failed to demonstrate so far.

> Queen **O me, what hast thou done?**
> Hamlet   **Nay, I know not.**
> **Is it the King?**

I ask the last question like 'Do you have two lumps or three?' – as if his death or life were as important to me as that. I am sitting on a cloud of confidence since I am now a man and no longer a virgin, and, even if my act of penetration was blind, to say the least, I did it. At least I am no longer a woman, i.e. *a very drab, / A scullion* [II, ii].

> Queen   **O what a rash and bloody deed is this!**
> Hamlet   **A bloody deed. Almost as bad, good mother,**
>   **As kill a king and marry with his brother.**

In a sense she is innocent of any crime but haste; but I must now unravel the gory plot.

> Queen   **As kill a king?**

Of course she is astonished at my revelation. I let it all out:

> Hamlet   **Ay, lady, it was my word. –**

I rush to the 'arras' with the confidence of a man who is about to exhibit his great masterpiece. I hope how to live in the fulfilment of my father's stern image. I pull open the 'arras' . . . and moan. Like . . . oh shit. Disappointment. What a bloody bore. But still I cannot allow this to diffuse my triumph. I have killed a defenceless old man, ruthlessly in the pursuit of my own potency, in the quest for manhood and revenge.

>   **Thou wretched, rash, intruding fool, farewell.**
>   **I took thee for thy better. Take thy fortune:**
>   **Thou find'st to be too busy is some danger. –**

Then I close the curtains. I actually would close the curtains after *farewell* and then deliver the rest as if to myself. I closed them curtly, as if shutting up shop for the night. This would sometimes get a laugh for the very coldness and indifference I expressed, but I couldn't show any feeling now. I had suffered a momentary setback and had actually murdered another human being in cold blood. The acknowledgement of this would have crushed me. While I will spend a good portion of my life analysing whether *to be or not to be* I will not give a moment of time to snatching a life. I cannot let it affect me and I must keep the blood pumping, even if it has been momentarily satisfied.

Gertrude is horrified and I am still proud, strutting here and there in my new colours as Danish 'tearaway':

> Hamlet   **Leave wringing of your hands. Peace, sit you down,**

> **And let me wring your heart; for so I shall**
> **If it be made of penetrable stuff . . .**

I take her hands and twist her round and force her again on to the
floor – which would have been the bed had we had one.

> *Queen*   **What have I done, that thou dar'st wag thy tongue**
> **In noise so rude against me?**

I stand over her collapsed body and slowly deliver the full impact of
the speech whose contents must go down clearly and surely:

> *Hamlet*   **Such an act**
> **That blurs the grace and blush of modesty,**
> **Calls virtue hypocrite, takes off the rose**

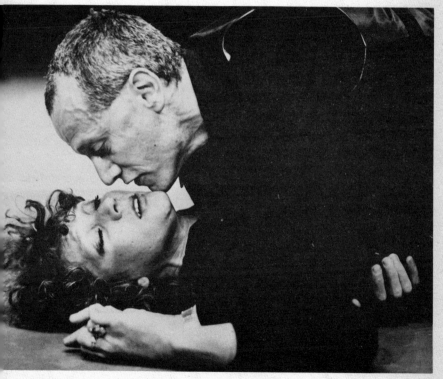

'O, tis most sweet / When in one line two crafts directly meet.' A little symbolism
squeezed into that one.

> **From the fair forehead of an innocent love**
> **And sets a blister there . . .**

I point to the centre of her forehead as if the mark of Cain was writ
large on her head. I take the speech only to *dicers' oaths*, which makes
the point aptly and clearly. To say any more will only confuse the
audience and make them wonder what Gertrude means when she
replies:

> *Queen*   **Ay me, what act . . . ?**

For some reason I seized her by the hair with my left hand while she
held my wrist; so I gave the impression that I was twisting her around
by her hair. I then held her chin with my right hand so as to show her
her 'act' and rub her nose in the shit of her own actions as if she were a
dog.

Now for the pictures of the King and Ghost . . .

Usually I have seen this situation dealt with by an actor fumbling
with a locket around his throat, or struggling with a locket around her
throat and comparing the two – it is usually a messy action. Now for
the advantage of our poor, or rather streamlined theatre, which
continually relies on the imaginative powers of the audience. This can
produce odd bonuses. Since the actors are on stage – Claudius sitting
on one side and the Ghost on the other – the two have only to turn
their bodies to face the stage to become real-life portraits.

Linda Marlowe (Gertrude) is on the floor making ladders in her
stockings while revealing plenty of her leg in her split-sided skirt.

> *Hamlet*   **Look here upon this picture, and on this,**

I drag her by her head to one and then the other, like a man possessed
and highly dangerous and wanting by this harsh action to make her
see and feel the extent of her 'crime', as if in some way to punish her.
So I make her look at the evidence, treating her like a rag doll:

> **The counterfeit presentment of two brothers.**

Still gripping the back of her head by her mane of hair, I guide her
face to one or other as the words suit. I extol the King's – my father's
– qualities. I am rapturous; my free right hand indicates the noble
face as if my own hand were carving out the features.

> **See what a grace was seated on this brow,**

Gertrude and Hamlet, as Hamlet forces her to compare the two men in her life. Roger Morton's picture captures an interesting mesh of hands.

For a moment my rapture has made me leave Gertrude and almost pray before the model of idealized fatherhood. Dad can do no wrong. All children know that.

> **A station like the herald Mercury**
> **New-lighted on a heaven-kissing hill,**

Perhaps this was the only time I expressed such passion to my father or his image; but the passion is still being fed from the deeper streams that were set in motion by a corpse whose blood is still oozing out as I rhapsodize about Dad. I finish my eulogy:

This was your husband.
Arm outstretched on *this*, as if, 'How could you think of anything less
to mate with?'

Look you now what follows.
I tear across the stage like an ice-skater, pointing at the opposite side
to Claudius; then turn away and vomit, or make a sound resembling
it:

Here is your husband, (*Retch.*)
It is so outrageous that it makes the audience laugh. Maybe it is too
much; but I'm still riding on the wings of murder:

like a mildew'd ear
Blasting his wholesome brother.
Somehow the effect of the two live statues brought the scenes to life in
the minds of the audience who could now actually compare the two
figures. I returned to Gertrude, still on the floor, centre stage.

Have you eyes?
Could you on this fair mountain leave to feed
And batten on this moor?
Once more I use her cruelly, twisting her round from left to right. It
appears to be more cruel than it is since Linda is still holding my wrist
and she actually controls the movement. She doesn't wish to look and
I force her to. I speak to her directly, eye to eye:

You cannot call it love; for at your age
The heyday in the blood is tame, it's humble,
And waits upon the judgment, and what judgment
Would step from this to this?
Again I lift her almost off the floor, but then I release her to complete
the speech:

Sense sure you have,
Else could you not have motion, but sure that sense
Is apoplex'd . . .
Eyes without feeling, feeling without sight,
Ears without hands or eyes,
I never grasped fully the last sentence but felt that I knew it
instinctively – that the senses were isolated and alienated without the

tempering qualities of other senses. Senses have to work with their opposites.

>   smelling sans all,
>   Or but a sickly part of one true sense
>   Could not so mope.

Here I changed *Or* to *All* and left out, rightly or wrongly, the obscure *Could not so mope*. Left as it was I referred to crotch power – that's the only part she could think with; and since *O shame, where is thy blush?* follows on, it seemed to be the right interpretation.

>   If thou canst mutine in a matron's bones,
>   To flaming youth let virtue be as wax
>   And melt in her own fire;

If an old bag can be abandoned, let youth be even more so since youth has the heat of passion at the same time.

Now some gestures are almost done subliminally – in fact most arrive from some unconscious desire when the words have truthfully trapped the impulses of the body. If this is resisted, the energy may find its way into the inflexion and colour of the words, but in any case this subtext will out. So I found myself undoing my waistcoat on *melt in her own fire* – like a man getting on with a 'quickie', getting his clothes off in a hurry for something that won't take long. Obviously I had no intention of screwing my mother but was making her into a symbol of woman in general. Also it might have had the appearance of turning up my cuffs before a fight. Gertrude must have read it as a threat. I did the gesture quite unconsciously and I let it be read by the audience in what way they would.

I am building up to the grand climax and this scene leads stage by stage to the most inexorable and dramatic series of climaxes; to an almost orgasmic conclusion.

> *Queen*   O Hamlet, speak no more.
>   Thou turn'st my eyes into my very soul,
>   And there I see such black and grained spots
>   As will not leave their tinct.

My words and gestures are getting through to her and helping her to convince herself of her own deeds. I have turned her eyes *into* her *very soul*, and that may be enough; but I want to revel in it and to torture myself with the image of her living –

 Hamlet **In the rank sweat of an enseamed bed,**

Now I become the judge and voyeur simultaneously. I am revolted and disgusted to a point I never imagined. How we start by the comparison of the two kings' qualities, and then get inside the bed imagining the stains! I am sickened as I imagine my mother being fucked by my uncle. My mother is not supposed to do such things. No boy's mother is. In the eyes of a child the mother is wholesome and pure and motherly, and by the time he becomes of an age to understand these things the mother has usually 'settled' into motherliness – especially given Hamlet's age: these things happened over twenty years ago. To stir up these ancient vaults now is more than Hamlet can bear. Fucking is what Hamlet does. The dirty sordid guilty thing that lies between his legs is a secret to his mother, as his mother's thing is to him. But now she is 'doing' what Hamlet does. Also, by a remarriage, she becomes closer to him since they are both afflicted by carnal desire. Suddenly she is young again, i.e. fuckable. Oh horror:

  Stew'd in corruption, honeying and making love
  Over the nasty sty!

Of course, in some ways Claudius represents the real carnal father who does dirty things to Mum, and the Ghost is the idealized spirit, the noble Mercury, Jupiter, all in the air and not tainted by the smell of sex. I am also crazy with a grief that has seeped into my anger. I'd even make the word *love* dirty by lolling my tongue out on the word and ululating it like some horny Greek porter – or a snake.

 Queen   **O speak to me no more.**
  These words like daggers enter in my ears.
  No more, sweet Hamlet.

My anger and jealousy and hate are streaming out and re-forming me, leaner and clearer and purged of these demons. But I have to go on. I have to push myself to the ultimate, whatever it is. Pretence of madness has touched real madness. Just as an actor corrupts himself with the role he is feigning and must become it by a process of identification, so am I in danger of tearing myself apart. I want to explode in total identification with my father; to kill; to push this experience to its ultimate conclusion. What more can I dredge up? Comparisons, sexual disgust, and now character assassination:

> *Hamlet*   **A murderer and a villain,**
> **A slave that is not twentieth part the tithe**
> **Of your precedent lord, a vice of kings,**
> **A cutpurse of the empire and the rule,**
> **That from a shelf the previous diadem stole**
> **And put it in his pocket –**

I heave the speech out of my body as if I was vomiting it out of my system and being cleansed in the process. I concertina my chest into a bellow, squeezing the choice nouns out: *murderer . . . villain . . . cutpurse*. I mime a thief stealing a precious thing and like a dirty Fagin I open my coat and sneak it in.

> *Hamlet*   **A king**

And here I pause, as if to trowel up the worst filth from my exposed sewers:

> **of shreds and patches –**

I knew that *patches* was to be my last yelp. I couldn't have gone on any more. Since I knew that the Ghost must rise and appear I could throw the last ounce I had on my final punch. I collapsed on seeing the Ghost.

He rises simply from the chair where he has been 'frozen' for the last twenty minutes. The *patches* get hooked on to this vision, and the word entangles itself on the shock as the Ghost comes to warn me that I am overreaching myself. I am becoming blunted, wallowing in the role the Ghost has given me. He appointed me as avenging angel and I have committed the worst crime attributed to the players: I have sawn *the air too much*. I have ranted, screamed, play-acted and generally indulged in my part, and like the good director the Ghost steps out of the shadows to give me a warning. I am totally spent, and in that moment I feel as if I have stepped out of Berkoff and become Hamlet. I want to avenge myself on society and then dress myself in his clothes. 'Society' is Claudius who has stepped into my shoes, contained me and threatened me and I seize on each raw wound and expose it as the result of society's fear of the non-conformist. I lay there, soaked in the pure sweat of my vengeance, purged at last of the passion that was unable to express itself in the cold-blooded English tradition, the frightened and luke-warm temperament, so unlike the Elizabethan. Every stab I made, every howl, was one more thrust into the great belly of British slothful indifference. I don't know why I thought of this now, but any interpreter will naturally fuel his vehicle from the tank of his own frustrations.

The Ghost walks towards me. I watch, eyes staring out of my head, back arched in fear, hair on end.

Wolf Kahler as the Ghost

Wolf had a special walk. His lantern jaw and wide blue eyes, fist forehead and sepulchral expression carved themselves into the light. He walked as if on wheels, body jutting forward and his arms hanging loosely down by his sides. I have worked with Wolf since 1973, when he worked with us on *Agamemnon*. He has an imposing demeanour, and moves as if obeying secret messages from deep within his psyche. Consequently his movement has none of the dull predictability of conventional modern acting where you can recognize the same armoury of moves. Even actors acknowledge this – that they are caught in some inescapable web of tradition – since they will often say, 'This is my "bemused" or "tragic" expression, pose 3a', for example. Wolf seems to be obeying commands that his conscious mind seems scarcely aware of. Consequently you will not see the familiar gestures that are faithfully recorded and reproduced by the conscious mind – like reproduction furniture.

The same goes for directing and staging, since we are talking about that. Nearly all productions have been observed before and are reproduced with tiny bits of icing sugar, such as some imaginative lighting or a bit of sound effect. This dead theatre poses as new in each case, but the excavations have not even started. Light and sound tend to reach the non-verbal – to strike chords deeper within us – and so 'directors' play with this to help the dull pill go down.

148

As for Wolf, who started me thinking about this, his improvisations in *Agamemnon* when we were working out the chorus shape were always unique and interesting to watch. Perhaps they were more intimate and closer to the real stress of battle. He would scan the fresco of bodies and sculpt himself into the exact place. Although rather typically German – if we are to refer to the archetype etched into our minds of one seeking order – and desiring to know months ahead of time the rehearsal schedule, and fazed if his chair was a few inches off the spot where it should have been, he nevertheless had a total vocal and physical freedom; perhaps because he was so disciplined and knew that the structure was secure, enabling him to be all the freer. So it seemed as if he had one part of his soul in heaven and the other half in order and constraint, but one half would inspire the other.

So, in this production, his 'resting' or watching positions as chorus were never those of casual watcher. His were careful, apposite, and instinctively right for the scene. When he was with us the cast felt more assured, for that very control and iron discipline which could switch and fuel great rage. He was a loner, even to the extent of travelling alone rather than face the chitchat of a group of actors in a train for an endless journey.

So there I was on the floor, twisted into shape as if I was fearing some retribution for having abused my mother; and his wife:

Hamlet   **Save me and hover o'er me with your wings,**
         You heavenly guards! What would your gracious figure?
Ghost   **Do not forget. This visitation**
         Is but to whet thy almost blunted purpose.
         But look, amazement on thy mother sits.
         O step between her and her fighting soul.
         Conceit in weakest bodies strongest works.
         Speak to her, Hamlet.

And he doesn't want me just to say, 'Hallo, Mum.' He means that my behaviour has hurt him and is straying from the purpose. He passes by me and I shrink as if expecting a blow or worse from him, as if a naughty child were expecting punishment. But he passes steadily on:

Hamlet **How is it with you, lady?**

Said simply, like 'Have a nice day.' I am quite shameless in being able to pull a line into any situation if I think there can be something mined from it; where the contrast between two opposing situations will bring about a humorous response: from the traumatic scene with Mum, to the mind-bending visitation of the Ghost, the pathetic descent to 'How are you?' caused a ripple through the audience which also helped to dispel the danger of over-seriousness. She responds:

Queen   **Alas, how is't with you . . . ?**

I watch the Ghost going off into the wings, and I am still shaking with fear and shock:

Queen   . . . **Whereon do you look?**

I cut the next speech and dive straight into:

Hamlet **Do you see nothing there?**

We don't need that speech of Hamlet about his father once again extolling his dad's virtues. Enough is enough, already.

Hamlet **Nor did you nothing hear?**

What I heard in fact was the low hum of the chorus; a slow soft deep 'Aaaaaahm' that followed and introduced the Ghost in all his appearances. The contrast between this steady and almost subliminal sound and the silence that was left in the air when it stopped was astonishing. It hung like a pall –

Hamlet **Look where he goes even now out at the portal.**

I run after the figure, sliding across the stage and snatching at space. Now you see him. Now you don't. My hands go through thin air as if I am snatching at something that I feel is corporeal. I turn suddenly, as if the full import of his presence is for the first time making itself felt – just as quickly as the heat raised in the confrontation with Gertrude is losing its value. I am afraid.

Queen **This is the very coinage of your brain.**

            This bodiless creation ecstasy

            Is very cunning in.

Now is the time when the feigning of madness works against me. I am

now hoist with my own petard, so when truth is patently there I will
not be believed. I must try to convince her of my sanity.

> *Hamlet* Ecstasy?
>> **My pulse as yours doth temperately keep time,**
>> **And makes as healthful music.**

Hardly now I would have thought! 'Ecstasy' I splutter, thrusting a
right arm out and snatching the wrist from its sleeve as if to test the
normality of my blood pressure. I do the action first, investing it with
the possibility of an aggressive gesture which becomes rationalized by
speech:

> *Hamlet*   **Mother, for love of grace,**
>> **Lay not that flattering unction to your soul,**
>> **That not your trespass but my madness speaks.**

I like the following lines, which I poured out like a wine into her as
she knelt, almost receiving them as a benediction as I stood, with
knees half bent, hovering over her. Deliberately and slowly I poured
the horrible corruption in the vials of her ears. I felt like a doctor who,
having lanced the boil and drawn the contents, shows the patient the
foul mess. 'God! was that inside me?' he may well ask on viewing the
wretched purulence. So Gertrude is witnessing her own corruption in
Hamlet the surgeon's eyes:

>> **It will but skin the film the ulcerous place,**
>> **Whiles rank corruption mining all within,**
>> **Infects unseen.**

But now it is a warning: a prophylactic against the danger of a far
worse disease. No more flailing now. Be clear, accurate, sincere.
Anyway, the Ghost may be watching, ready to come out and spring
on me. I dart anxious glances around the room. I stand over her like a
sentinel now, take her two agitated hands and place them together in
prayer – or, more likely, as an indication of what she must do. My
hands are over hers.

>> **Confess yourself to heaven,**
>> **Repent what's past, avoid what is to come;**

(The body has been forgotten about, still bleeding freely behind the
curtain.)

> **And do not spread the compost on the weeds**
> **To make them ranker.**

I am pleading now, almost in tears for her human frailty – particularly on *avoid what is to come*. By now Gertrude, having suffered the juiciest images I can summon up, must be feeling like a leprous whore:

Queen **O Hamlet, thou hast cleft my heart in twain.**

I again stoop into the pit for a nasty laugh and deliver:

Hamlet **O throw away the worser part of it**

as if I said it to someone who had burnt a cake and was trying to salvage some of it. Said simply and cynically it invites laughter again at the contrast between her passion and Hamlet's sarcasm. Also he is by no means won over by her heartfelt metaphors:

> **And live the purer with the other half.**

They are good lines, and should be stated boldly and simply.

Many of Hamlet's lines have a biblical quality to them which gives Hamlet a Messianic fervour at times. Certainly a man of great moral fibre, and one through whom we test the corruption of the times: 'If thine eye offend thee, pluck it out' could be *throw away the worser part of it*. He could be a preacher advising us and exhorting us to respect the sanctity of life. Hamlet the Messiah – for so the play seems as we tour Europe with our twelve disciples, armed with our play of Christian and humanistic ethics – an adventure story carefully concealing a profound, moving philosophy. A human being is pitted against the pursy corruption of his times and sacrificed like Jesus for daring to speak and fight against it. Betrayed by Judas/Laertes.

ON OUR LAST TOUR OF EUROPE THERE WAS A RUMOUR THAT THE MESSIAH WAS ABOUT TO APPEAR. IT WAS HIS TIME TO COME AND SOMEONE CLAIMED TO HAVE SEEN HIM IN THE EAST END OF LONDON! ONE DAY ON THE TRAIN, IDLY LETTING MY MIND GO ITS OWN WAY, I DISCOVERED THAT IN OUR CAST OR COMPANY WERE EXACTLY THIRTEEN PEOPLE INCLUDING MYSELF: NINE ACTORS, ONE MUSICIAN, AND THREE STAGE-MANAGERS. A MAGIC NUMBER. THEN, PLAYING AROUND WITH THE IDEA MORE FULLY, LAERTES

WAS A JUDAS, CLAUDIUS A PILATE, AND POLONIUS THE FISHER-MAN. THE GHOST WAS A SPIRIT OF GOD INSTRUCTING ME AND SENDING ME DOWN TO DO HIS WILL. GERTRUDE WAS THE VIRGIN MARY, AND OPHELIA, MARY MAGDALENE. THE PLAYERS WERE THE CHILDREN THAT JESUS LOVED, AND HAMLET'S SOLILOQUIES WERE SERMONS TO THE PEOPLE. HAMLET WAS CERTAINLY A JESUS FIGURE – SOMEONE WHO MUST BE SACRIFICED FROM TIME TO TIME TO REMIND THE WORLD WHEN IT STRAYS FROM THE PATH OF VIRTUE OR EXCELLENCE; AS IF THE WORLD THROWS UP THESE 'PURER SPECIMENS' THAT IT WORSHIPS AND ADORES BUT SOME-HOW HAS TO DESTROY, SINCE THE CONSTANT LIGHT IS TOO MUCH, BUT THEN CAN MOURN THE LOSS LATER.

Now the strange thing is that one found reflections of this within the group. As people got into their characters they tended to sleep in them. Hamlet was betrayed by Laertes who, like Judas, was once his ally, and Horatio was always his ally in a way like John the Baptist. In any great work one sees the struggle between two forces of light and darkness, if you like, and the shades of grey between; the audience or reader is gathered somehow from his slumbers in the nether region and encouraged to climb to the top and see the view. The members of the audience are almost like floating voters who wish to be inspired and delivered from themselves into a collective force. In the struggle of the forces the martyr arises who is born of the struggle and who then guides it until his eventual destruction. He is invariably destroyed since, once he is discovered, he is then 'claimed' – so the same struggle that would forge Jesus would forge Hamlet. Both are in a sense shaped by the very hostility around them. They become a mould which the forces of the world try to crush.

Looking at it this way, we found all sorts of coincidences which fitted this view; e.g.

Polonius **Do you know me, my lord?**
Hamlet **Excellent well. You are a fishmonger.** [II, ii]

We have mentioned this, but Polonius in the shape of David Auker – round, bucolic and sometimes alcoholic – was indeed like a fisher of souls. Young as he was, he would always give counsel within the group and console where necessary. Also he offered advice to Laertes in the form of ten commandments. I counted them one day, and indeed there are ten. This was one of the many backgrounds against which the play could be viewed and, like an ever-moving spectrum, it seemed to adjust itself to whatever the situation demanded. But there is only one and that is the one you choose or that chooses you.

Hamlet **Good night.**

I linger here to say the unspeakable. I cannot look at her when I say the following. I hold her hand but struggle with

But go not to my uncle's bed.

It is an imploring child in the centre and an adult on the outside. Of course you mustn't sleep with a murderer and a villain, but I haven't actually said Claudius killed Hamlet. I have implied it in anger but offered no proof. All I have done is make comparison between the two men. Therefore, much as I may personally resent Claudius for whatever good reason, I have offered no proof other than my set of values for his worthlessness. Therefore to implore my mother not to go to bed with him must seem impudent to her, to say the least. But not if the relationship has somehow shifted its focus! Somehow the mother–son relationship is taking on a different hue. It is becoming a touch intimate; even a whisper incestuous!

Assume a virtue if you have it not.

More like a retort to an out-of-favour lover than to a mother with whom we don't even like doing such monstrous things.

Refrain tonight,
And that shall lend a kind of easiness
To the next abstinence, the next more easy;
For use almost can change the stamp of nature . . .

Am I giving a lesson in chastity or do I really crave my mother's bed? I kiss her on the cheek as I say:

I must be cruel only to be kind.
This bad begins, and worse remains behind.

I leave, but turn as if as an afterthought. I look at her . . . she is dishevelled . . . still on the floor (bed) . . . skirt riding up . . .

154

careless in the distress of the moment . . . flushed and abused. Something has started in the intimacy that rage produces to break down the formalities between mother and son; something in the fury of the hate revealed the underbelly of desire . . .

So, again, good night.

I kiss her again and stroke her hair that I had so rudely pulled around. I am in utter remorse for what I have done. I attempt to justify my act: *I must be cruel only to be kind. / This bad begins, and worse remains behind*. I linger, still unfulfilled but almost bathed in this newfound flow of remorse which has also triggered off some strange feelings of affection. I idle in the atmosphere that we have created, as if reluctant to leave. There's a smell in the air which is explosive . . . I don't want to leave . . . there is something unfulfilled. If I open the door and leave now there will never again be the combination of events to create this particular atmospheric stew. I have abused my mother, killed my first victim, been visited by a ghost, and nearly brought myself to the point of killing my uncle and – apart from directing my first thriller – it has been a spectacular night. How can I end it now? So I drift in the room, my shirt pulled awry, sweat still smearing my face; she, lipstick-smudged and generally looking thoroughly dishevelled and whorish; in the background the blood trickling through from behind the 'arras' from Polonius's still-warm body . . . and the King somewhere below no doubt, fulminating and on his way. It's all too sickly sweet to go . . . *something more must happen*.

Hamlet   **One word more, good lady.**

I cannot go and idle the time until I have fulfilled whatever it is that is unspoken between us which has been brought to the surface by these events. I have said goodnight twice and still linger. She looks at me. I am using the King to express something else. Is he becoming accidentally the fulcrum on which we turn? She asks:

Queen   **What shall I do?**

I begin:

Hamlet   **Not this, by no means, that I bid you do:**

Now I use the King for my illustration. I will become a certain director who, in order to get a closer proximity to a desirable actress, uses the part of the 'role' to seize hold of her, so under the guise of art he enjoys her proximity which could not be enjoyed otherwise without offence – the art somehow nullifies the intention. I thus advise Gertrude by impersonating the King, so no offence will be construed under the game. I am acting, and if, during the act, I feel some response, then I slowly remove the 'prop' of the game. I pull her down to the floor.

> **Let the bloat King tempt you again to bed,**
> **Pinch wanton on your cheek, call you his mouse,**

(Now I am getting on top of her, getting into character . . .)

> **And let him, for a pair of reechy kisses . . .**

(nearly mouth to mouth)

> **Make you to ravel all this matter out**
> **That I essentially am not in madness,**
> **But mad in craft. 'Twere good you let him know . . .**

The rest of this obscure stuff you can safely cut, lest you spoil a very good meal. So I have contradicted myself: in one moment I have begged her not to go near him – with the most persuasive argument I can muster – and now I am saying do the opposite, and tell the King that I am *mad in craft*. What for? In other words, I am not mad; let the King fear for his life and know that I am on to him. Or is it . . . ? Gertrude answers lamely:

> *Queen*　　　　　　　　 **. . . if words be made of breath,**
> **And breath of life, I have no life to breathe**
> **What thou hast said to me.**

I ignore this cute circumlocution and hang about a bit more. There is a silence. What else can regenerate our proceedings? I have to get the spark going again. The desire is fading . . . the sweat is drying on our faces and I should be saying *Good night, mother* for the third time unless I can think of something. The scene has already been going for twenty minutes . . . I can only think of a negative piece of chat:

> *Hamlet*　 **I must to England, you know that?**

As if I had said, 'I've given up smoking, you know that?' She answers more lamely than ever:

> *Queen*　　　　　　　　　　　　　　 **Alack,**

156

I had forgot. 'Tis so concluded on.

She had forgot because she never knew. Nobody has told her. Shakespeare has just thought it up. Now, having used the King to charge the adrenalin, I turn to the two adders who will escort me to England:

    Hamlet   **There's letters seal'd, and my two schoolfellows,**
           Whom I will trust as I will adders fang'd –
           They bear the mandate . . .

My heat is returning as I am inspired again. Somehow I can act only if something else not necessarily related provokes me. I am still over the Queen; lying not quite on top but casually draped over her. In this position I must speak. There cannot be too much silence lest we discover where we are!

           [They] marshal me to knavery. Let it work;

I add, as if, 'Let them try and see where it gets them . . .' Now, in my excitement, I become aware of my position straddling the Queen. Now I am proving to her I am a man.

           For 'tis the sport to have the enginer
           Hoist with his own petard,

I take her wrists and thrust them down behind her as if to ravish my sweetheart. I feel her beneath me but she doesn't withdraw or twist away but stays as a cushion of flesh for my desire which is delivered via my anger for Rosencrantz and Guildenstern. I grind my words and my body into her and she accepts both. This outrage to her is neatly doubled by my hatred:

                      and't shall go hard
           But I will delve one yard below their mines
           And blow them at the moon.

I am full in the flush of my desire again, somehow unable to separate hate and lust but letting the two weave together, the one supporting the other. I sing the word *blow*. It would come out as if my very breath put them into vertical ascent and they would be borne aloft. Now more doors are opening. How easy it is to match a metaphor with a crude physical – i.e. sexual – connotation; but here they are irresistible to me: we are bone to bone and one line stimulates the next. I have arched my back on *blow them at the moon* as if for me this is the climax, my orgasmic thrust into space, the full load of my lust and fury racing to the surface and exploding. And then on the down beat:

O, 'tis most sweet
When in one line two crafts directly meet.

I relish the words *sweet*, *crafts*, still holding her by the wrists but now dying away. But as I ram the words of killing into her ears and the passion into her body I felt that my secret was not unacknowledged. It is over – for my body it is over. I can no longer bear to be where I am. I climb off –

Good night, mother.

– like a client leaving his whore. Then I see the body which we had both conveniently forgotten about; and now there might be an unfortunate bloody puddle. I do not imply that anything has happened which was untoward, except I pull down her skirt which has ridden up.

I'll lug the guts into the neighbour room.

She is still on the floor, watching me leave, and sharing our little bloody encounter in her heart:

This counsellor
Is now most still, most secret, and most grave,
Who was in life

And here I would pause, as if searching for the appropriate rhyme:

a foolish prating knave.

I would chortle at my own wit while searching her eyes for approval.

Come, sir, to draw toward an end with you.

I would lift the ample arms of Polonius and drag him a yard, whereupon Polonius would get up as the actor who had finished his task and had no need merely to be a body. I now, having established to the audience the fact of dragging the corpse, mime it.

Now, for the very last time:

Good night, mother.

The Chorus

Polonius, of course, no longer exists, but doesn't have to sit in a dressing room and play Scrabble until the curtain call. His able and creative body will serve many other purposes, thus enabling us to stage *Hamlet* with ten actors.

I am now away and out of the room. Polonius has joined the group belonging to the King and strangely I no longer recognize him as Polonius; nor does it occur to anyone that he shouldn't be on stage. These discriminations belong to consumer theatre where realism borders on the simplistic acceptance of a staged event as real.

In traditional theatre where the actor reflected the economic and social conditions of the time, the actor was a servant to the star, who was the 'capitalist' with the most lines and time. The peon served only as decoration and was divested of all skill except that of being a body. How many of you can remember actors standing at the back for countless minutes in a Shakespeare revival while the 'lead' speaks? And the minutes seem like hours. How many of you have seen them looking bored out of their heads and occasionally making unctuous little smiles as the king or prince wallows on . . . while at the same time shifting the weight of their under-used bodies, facing front in their expensive costumes and 'looking' like a crowd. But never used, in the real sense of being there? Of course all of you, especially critics, have seen this. A dreadful waste of human material. After a while we accept the dreary tradition like the king who wore no clothes, and dutifully attempt to ignore the sorry waste of human spirit and material. The actors too accept this awful conspiracy of mediocrity and feel their lives onstage depend only on playing good or leading parts. Most directors are really interested only in the leading actors, leaving the rest of the crowd somehow to fit in with no sense of purpose. If they become a little problematic, a 'movement person' is brought in to deal with them and make a little flurry of activity. Such events are usually masques and balls . . . a little awkward acrobatics or court dances.

ACT IV

SCENE I

I go off and now the King is on his way, but we decided to bring in the whole court. I am seen to be dangerous and mad so it is natural that they should come in. The King enters alone at first. I am trying to remember but my feeling is that there was a flurry of movement round the stage suggesting still the unrest in the castle, whispers in corridors, fleeing courtiers, etc. This all takes place while Gertrude lies on the floor, thus compressing the two images. As the people withdraw we suddenly see the King.

King   **What, Gertrude, how does Hamlet?**
Queen   **Mad as the sea and wind when both contend**
Which is the mightier. In his lawless fit,
Behind the arras hearing something stir,
Whips out his rapier, cries 'A rat, a rat',
And in this brainish apprehension kills
The unseen good old man.

So, having just said to me, *if words be made of breath, / And breath of life, I have no life to breathe / What thou hast said to me*, how quickly she leaps to her own defence!

King   **O heavy deed!**
It had been so with us [me] had we [I] been there.

And now begins the conspiracy to get rid of me. Gertrude is still lying there while Claudius paces up and down:

King   **. . . we will ship him hence, and this vile deed**
We must with all our majesty and skill
Both countenance and excuse. – Ho, Guildenstern!

The whole court now comes streaming in the doors – the first two men of course becoming the double doors of the room and the cast pouring through until the doors themselves dissolve and enter the room. It is like a stream of flesh pouring through: I want to suggest panic and fear rather than just have Rosencrantz and Guildenstern enter.

They are all now in the room. Gertrude has now risen and is attempting to pull herself together.

    King   **Hamlet in madness hath Polonius slain . . .**

Ophelia screams and faints into the arms of Horatio.

        Go, seek him out– speak fair – and bring the body
        Into the chapel. I pray you haste in this.

Rosencrantz and Guildenstern exit looking for me. The group remains frozen downstage.

SCENE II

I am in the corridor, or on the white line, upstage. I hear Rosencrantz and Guildenstern calling for me: 'Hamlet! Lord Hamlet!'

    Hamlet   . . . **O, here they come.**

The chase.

I wish to torment them. I am walking along the outer perimeter or the corridor and they follow me. I describe the square of the stage.

    Rosencrantz   **What have you done, my lord, with the dead**
        body?
    Hamlet   **Compounded it with dust whereto 'tis kin.**
    Rosencrantz   **Tell us where 'tis, that we may take it thence**
        and bear it to the chapel.

The following speech, referring to them as sponges, I regretfully cut later in the run to save time and because we have dealt with my attitude towards them sufficiently in the scene with the pipe. In the early days when it was kept I would stop to tell them the 'ape' speech, then continue to walk. But suddenly I would break into a run. I would tear round corners with the two of them following me, skidding like a car on two wheels. It resembled for a few seconds a Charlie Chaplin short – the way he would corner on one hopping leg.

Both Rosencrantz and Guildenstern did the same. Hamlet was having a game! So it was very appropriate. John Prior, our musician, accompanied us on the piano, sounding like an old-fashioned two-reeler. It was very funny and welcome relief after two hours. It could have been the Keystone Cops as they tried to catch me. I mimed going up the stairs and they followed me. Reaching the top of the stairs I found a 'door' and opened it, locking myself inside. They crashed into my mimed door. We continued the conversation with them outside the chamber. Of course, this would be a natural way of doing it if we were filming it. I lay on the floor in a relaxed pose:

> *Rosencrantz*   **My lord, you must tell us where the body is**
>   **and go with us to the King.**
>
> *Hamlet*   (*Lying down and smoking a cigarette* à la *Noël*)
>   **The body is with the King, but the King is not**
>   **with the body. The King is a thing –**
>
> *Guildenstern*   **A thing, my lord?**
>
> *Hamlet*   **Of nothing. Bring me to him.**

I now open the door which they had been crouching against and say:

> **Hide fox, and all after.**

And run away again. This time they split up and trap me. I am taken to the entrance of the King's chamber. The cast are where we left them a couple of moments ago. The King is finishing his speech. Rosencrantz and Guildenstern wait with me.

SCENE III

We wait because the King must make a speech. Since he cannot be waiting in Gertrude's bedroom we must shift the scene to allow the next actors on stage, who then use the stage for whatever purpose they designate. In order to facilitate this an actor has usually to say 'Come, away', or something similar. In our case we do not lose the presence of Claudius but let him remain on stage while the scene of Hamlet plus Rosencrantz and Guildenstern takes place around him.

165

Claudius comes to life. We have come to his room where he holds court and conducts affairs of state. Claudius finishes his speech with:

King   **Diseases desperate grown**
         By desperate appliance are reliev'd,
         Or not at all.

Rosencrantz comes in and explains that Hamlet is outside but they don't know the whereabouts of the corpse and I am brought in. I must continue the 'act' in front of the King and the others. I'm given the opportunity to ridicule the King and he becomes a simple butt for some more gallows humour.

Hamlet and Claudius.

It has been a very long first half and so much has happened in the last half-hour. We are exhausted and I am soaking in sweat. Guildenstern drags me before Claudius with one arm behind my back. I feel like a bad boy who has been brought before the headmaster for a caning. Ophelia breaks loose and tries to claw my eyes out but is held back – just. I am dishevelled and dirty and my shirt hangs out; I look totally mad. They are all watching me with a mixture of fascination and disgust. I face the object of my loathing: Claudius, alias Matthew Scurfield. His head is shaved bald and he reminds me of a gargoyle on Notre Dame. He also looks like a devil. He faces me calmly and speaks:

Claudius   **Now, Hamlet, where's Polonius?**
Hamlet   **At supper.**
Claudius   **At supper? where?**

(He looks round to share with the guests a knowing look – a 'we must humour him' look.)

Hamlet   **Not where he eats, but where a is eaten. A**
              certain convocation of politic worms are e'en at him.
              Your worm is your only emperor for diet; we fat all
              creatures else to fat us, and we fat ourselves for maggots.
              Your fat king and your lean beggar is but variable
              service – two dishes, but to one table. That's the end.
Claudius   **Alas, alas!**

166

(He feels very satisfied to see me so cuckoo.)

    Hamlet **A man may eat fish with the worm that hath eat of a
        king, and eat of the fish that hath fed of that worm.**

    Claudius (*Smiling, to a dolt*) **What dost thou mean by this?**

    Hamlet (*Final and hard*) **Nothing** . . .

I paused after *Nothing*, which received a laugh since my convoluted
speech had gone nowhere, then picked up the rest of the sentence:

        **. . . but to show you how a king may go a progress
        through the guts of a beggar.**

Here I sometimes was tempted to illustrate simply how he enters my
mouth: using my forefinger I traced a line down my chest demon-
strating the route the king will go until he exits as shit. Rather gross!
Especially if I let out a large raspberry at the end! But since I am mad
it does allow a certain amount of licence.

    Claudius **Where is Polonius?**

    Hamlet **In heaven.**

(Of course Claudius's part has been unfairly underwritten here to
demonstrate Hamlet's raging wit; Claudius is the straight man.)

        **Send thither to see. If your messenger find him not
        there, seek him i'th'other place yourself. (***Laughs.***)
        But if indeed you find him not within this month** . . .

(I pinch my nose which simultaneously suggests Polonius's stinking
carcass and makes the sound of a Harrods lift attendant.)

        **. . . you shall nose him as you go up the stairs into the
        lobby.**

    Claudius **Go seek him there.**

    Hamlet **A will stay till you come.**

Hamlet has acted as a thoroughly naughty boy and must now be sent
into the corner – or to England, which is about the same.

    King **Hamlet, this deed, for thine especial safety –
        Which we do tender, as we dearly grieve
        For that which thou hast done – must send thee hence
        With fiery quickness. Therefore prepare thyself.
        The bark is ready, and the wind at help,
        Th'associates tend, and everything is bent**

> For England.
> *Hamlet*   **For England.**
> *Claudius*   **Ay, Hamlet.**

Hamlet, spoiled brat, hates the idea and grimaces; sees no other way out and says indifferently,

> *Hamlet*   **Good.**
> *Claudius*   **So is it, if thou knew'st our purposes.**

Is this a veiled threat or even an aside? I took it to be an aside that Hamlet's keen ear picks up, rather than a bold equivocal statement. It is too sinister to be made in even the most apparently harmless way.

> *Hamlet*   **I see a cherub that sees them.**

In other words, 'I can read your thoughts since you are so transparent'; but also, 'I am guarded by angels who will watch over me.' In other words, 'I am on to you.'

> *Hamlet*   **But come, for England. Farewell, dear mother.**
> *Claudius*   **Thy loving father, Hamlet.**

Could Shakespeare have intended an interval here, or is this the second interval? He is pulling out all stops and dredging himself of every pun, hitting the audience with an artillery of ideas and images in a way that suggests wanting them back for the next act after he has ended in his best fashion.

> *Hamlet*   **My mother. Father and mother is man and wife,**
> **man and wife is one flesh; so my mother. Come, for**
> **England.**

What I am saying is a direct quote, as we all know, from the Jewish Bible. Marriage binds two people together as one flesh, so Hamlet could be saying I am addressing the female part of you as if they (King and Queen) were Siamese twins. On the other hand, Claudius has obeyed another ancient Jewish law which holds a male responsible for the wife of a deceased brother, and he must marry her! This protects a single wife who has little chance of marrying again on a competitive open market.

   I turn away, since I feel a building of tension that allows no exit except through violence. There was a fury that was on the point of igniting and needed only a fractional increase of temperature to set a conflagration going. So I turn away for a second before this happens. Having brought the bull to charging point I step to one side and let him stew in his own juice. I see Matthew Scurfield's eyes almost turn in on themselves. Rarely wishing to hold my eyes, sometimes he would act inwardly as if an inferno were going on within himself.

I walk off and freeze-frame upon myself as if they are seeing me walk into the distance, and certainly they are seeing me in their minds.

Claudius is released from his bonds, and barks – once more the dictator:

> *King*　**Follow him at foot. Tempt him with speed aboard,**
> **Delay it not – I'll have him hence tonight.**
> **Away, for everything is seal'd and done**
> **That else leans on th'affair. Pray you, make haste.**

What joy; he's found his voice again. No more stupid insinuating backchat but only the sound of his own voice fuelled by the acid burning inside his guts. Now he plots my death in the full sweetness of the blood almost upon his lips.

On *Pray you, make haste*, the walk begins around the perimeter of the stage. Rosencrantz and Guildenstern follow me and the rest of the cast rises and follows them until we are a moving fresco of the court with Claudius in the middle following our progress with his eyes. He becomes the hub of the wheel around which we turn. He has, in effect, set all this in motion. The drum beats out our exit. Claudius comes to life in all his fury. Pointing to me with outstretched arm that might well be a javelin if, like an Egyptian magician, he could turn it into one and hurl it with all his might at my departing back. Even so, I feel the hatred as my image sits in his head like a tumour.

> *King*　　　　　　　　　　　　　　**Do it, England;**
> **For like the hectic in my blood he rages,**
> **And thou must cure me. Till I know 'tis done,**
> **Howe'er my haps, my joys were ne'er begun.**

The actors walk off and I lead into the welcoming dark recesses of peace and sweet relief, leaving the madman ranting alone on his empty stage. Oh, thank God. Darkness. Applause.

169

The Interval

If it has been good I turn to the actors streaming out behind me and say, 'Good one' . . . 'Well done.' The better I have been the more I congratulate the others. I am enthused and excited. As I go down the corridor I am already tearing my shirt off and the cooler air hits and caresses me. My shirt is usually soaking wet. (On one tour I had only one shirt that was in the style I liked and a bored stage management, resulting in our touring photographer Roger Morton ironing out the sweat in the interval. Good old Roger.) We all walk off with relief after hours. They may sometimes say something to me, 'Great, Steven' . . . 'You were very good tonight' – this would often come from David Meyer, one of the Meyer twins, playing Rosencrantz, and I would appreciate this feedback after that exhausting act. Occasionally Terry McGinity (Laertes) would also murmur encouragingly and then I knew that it really had been good since I knew that he, being a rather critical actor and a real potential Hamlet, was the last person to praise anyone. Matthew (Claudius) would be more rational and say, 'You were good . . . in places', 'The first speech was never better . . . you did a great player scene.' I would praise Laertes for a good opener, Horatio for a good 'greeting scene'. (That would be very special to me. Greetings on stage are wonderful events to act. I don't know why but they seem to allow you to express as much affection as you personally feel.) The closet scene with Gertrude, having been so worked out, was invariably successful on one level or another. I would always ask of Linda, 'How was it?' and she would always say, 'Excellent, it was wonderful tonight.' But if I felt I lacked the power or was tired and bemoaned the scene, she would counter by saying, 'It was different, but felt just as good.' It was something to feel at home in. To Ophelia I'd say, 'Good one.' Sally Bentley would reply, 'Yes, it felt very good', in a gentle and slightly earnest fashion. I never felt quite at home in that scene and sometimes felt quite awkward; but with Sally – our latest Ophelia – I certainly felt more at ease, and on the nights it worked I felt elated.

To have all the scenes in the first half work gave me an incredible feeling of control and centredness. Playing Hamlet makes you feel like a prize-fighter in a fairground, taking on all-comers. Each scene is a new opponent to be faced with new tricks up its sleeve. Another difficult territory to be navigated is the mind of the audience. Each one has its favourite routes; nearly everyone has a scene they remember well with one particular actor; each has a moment when Gielgud did this and Olivier was breathtaking in that. On tour in Israel one faced a multitude of races in one audience, each with their country of origin's favourite Hamlet. I remember the trepidation I felt after having lunch in the kibbutz canteen and being assaulted with descriptions of the great Komisarjevsky's Hamlet, or the great Max Reinhardt production. I had gone to Israel with no great expectations of any high critical demands being made on me. But, on the contrary, the demands were even greater there than elsewhere. There is no other play in the Shakespeare canon that is so much part of the consciousness of the audience. It was part of my consciousness, so why not of theirs?

Shortly after working in the BBC Christopher Plummer *Hamlet* I saw the talented Peter O'Toole's fey prince open at the National Theatre a few weeks later. I was reminded of how little the modern actor could compare with the great classical ones. A whole realm of shambling louts shat on Hamlet for the next decade. Plummer, under the direction of Tyrone Guthrie, was the beacon, along with Olivier of course. A bad time for hams. They all came, parading their spots as if they were jewels, and each one somehow worse than the other. It became a chore to go anywhere near a *Hamlet*, and yet director after director sought in *Hamlet* the affirmation of their newfound liberation. Each one dragged out yards of preciously retained dull text; each one had ordered his cannisters of dry ice for the Ghost scene where it would roll into the audiences who suspected they were being gassed. I think that the RSC has shares in dry-ice machines. I venture a theory that the sixties – if such a period can be defined – led people by the nose of sexual and social revolution. And if John Osborne could show us the dirty underwear of society, so could these directors who saw in Hamlet the Billy Liar or Jimmy Porter of the Elizabethans.

One winter we were playing *Hamlet* in a series of ghastly halls in Belgium and I was suffering terribly with a duodenal ulcer. The interval was the only time I could lie down and rest. I'd swallow some milk while Roger was finishing off the ironing of my soaking shirt and hope it would be almost dry. Then we'd hear the call and reassemble in the wings to go on. We had to get into the right order since we had to occupy certain chairs. There'd always be an element of fooling around and nervous horseplay. Horatio would fool around with the late Polonius and Matthew Scurfield would stand a little apart, looking very smart and devilish in his tails, with a shaft of light catching and bouncing off his bald shaven head. Linda was adjusting her costume, which was now a dress with a giant embroidered flower sewn across it. Her first-half two-piece suit with the slash to the thighs would inevitably have burst in several places from our exertions, and would be being repaired in time for the next show. Ophelia wore an old (Victorian) nightdress and looked suitably mad, and I wore an old navy raincoat of the kind that English children wear at public school. Terry McGinity, as Laertes, was now in a more intense state since he was winding himself up for his entrance and big scene. And so we all shuffled in line and then we heard the announcement of the drum: clear, ringing and plangent.

We walked in line like gladiators, ready to deal out death and mortal wounding in the second half. There was always an air of anticipation in the house when we returned. Not a shuffling like, 'How are we going to take any more?' but a real interest in what we had to offer now. There is something very special about playing in Europe, which any actor will tell you. There is a charge in the air and everyone seems to sit upright in his or her seat wanting to absorb all you have. We received our cue and marched on. How familiar it all is after a while; when once it was a pain in the head to decide how to direct or act a scene. Now we strode in with all the confidence of Houdinis, ready with our daring bundle of tricks. Our last performance was in a broiling studio in Paris in May 1982. It was Barrault's theatre, the Rond Point; he came back in the interval after the first half, congratulated us and apologized for not seeing the second half but he had to rush home to 'Madeleine', who had been suffering with flu . . . we naturally had to believe him.

SCENE IV

A plain in Denmark.

We all wandered on and sat down stage right, apart from the two pairs of men who sat stage left. A drum cracked and the lights came up. I watched as two men opposite climbed on to their partners' shoulders. They looked very stately and very much like thoroughbred horses. The height was extraordinary since they were about the same height as a horse. They slowly circled the stage, making very gentle movements of a rider holding his reins. This was of course Fortinbras and his captain. From our seated positions opposite we made appropriate sounds with our feet of the slow amble of horses' hoofs. They reached the centre of the stage after circling it:

Fortinbras   **Go, captain, from me greet the Danish king . . .**
(This time Wolf Kahler plays Fortinbras and he really looks most

173

stately on his horse, reminding me for a moment of the prince he
played in Kubrick's *Barry Lyndon*.)

    Captain   **I will do't, my lord.**

    Fortinbras   **Go softly on.**

As he finishes saying this I get up and walk down to them as if I have
just entered this valley. It is cold and I turn my collar up.

    Hamlet   **Good sirs, whose powers are these?**

I seem to stare up from a lowly position. I clutch a small case with my
travelling kit – no doubt just emergency snacks, etc. Another time I
might sling a camera over my shoulder. Anyway, this time the
Falklands War is on and bears an uncanny resemblance to what this
Captain is describing, and the evening feels very charged at this point
since one automatically interprets a play according to one's own
experience, and now the Falklands disaster is everybody's war:

    Captain   **We go to gain a little patch of ground**

           That hath in it no profit but the name.

           To pay five ducats – five – I would not farm it . . .

    Hamlet   **Two thousand souls and twenty thousand ducats**

           Will not debate the question of this straw!

           This is th'impostume of much wealth and peace . . .

To tell you the truth, I didn't like the word *impostume* and didn't use
these lines. I ended on the Captain's line, *Yes, it is already garrison'd*,
and then left a silence before lurching into:

    Hamlet   **How all occasions do inform against me,**

           And spur my dull revenge.

I cut the marvellous

                        What is a man

        If his chief good and market of his time

        Be but to sleep and feed? A beast, no more.

It is a brilliant comment and could fit into many other plays; it is a
fitting debate on our cowardice to act: how we are all guilty in the face
of some example that suddenly strikes us when we are suspended in
indecision. Well, to tell you the truth, the very thing that Hamlet is
describing here, he is doing. We are back in the mirror staring at our

warts, still mulching the old fodder. So I went straight into a strong declaration to the audience:

Witness this army

I dived right into their sympathies:

of such mass and charge . . .

I am in the now for a change, and not in the reflective mood. The audience sees the army and the prince and can relate to what is now, and not to a further deliberation and whitewashing of my impotence by quoting examples. Let's get on with it . . .

I must add that I have a tendency to exploit a situation for all it's worth if I feel I can justify it. Before starting my speech I searched my pockets and found some sugar for the horse and fed it to Gary Whelan as the Captain. This used to get a huge laugh but it was a laugh of acknowledgement for the joke that Hamlet was sharing with the audience. We cannot have unmitigated gloom. So I would pretend to feed sugar to the horse before they went on their way. It was a silly gesture but I felt it relieved the audience and they paid all the more attention to me after that since they felt that perhaps Hamlet was a man they could relate to and joke with, and certainly he was one of the people.

The horses go away slowly, in a stately fashion and eventually stop. The riders dismount, becoming chorus once more. I continue. The joker becomes angry:

. . . while to my shame I see
The imminent death of twenty thousand men. . .

I was angry and ashamed and my fury burst from me. I was ashamed to be part of a nation that was gung-ho for the war while the cheap nasty tabloids were spewing phrases like *GOTCHA!* when people were dying –

Even for an egg-shell.

But there was no honour in this war – the one in the Falklands where soon thousands would die or be horribly burnt by one woman's desire to unite her country and one man's desire to get a piece of his back. Whether his case was right or not we would see pointless death to regain a piece of rock *That hath in it no profit but the name* . . . well, I

175

suppose it had a great deal more. But for the poor sailors drowning in the *Belgrano*, and the faces burnt away in the *Sheffield*:

> **That, for a fantasy and trick of fame,**
> **Go to their graves like beds, fight for a plot . . .**
> **Which is not tomb enough and continent**
> **To hide the slain.**

When the company was in France at this time we would travel in our bus and Wolf would tell us the news coming over his radio. We would gasp at the meaningless stupidity and banality of it all. I think we became somehow sensitized by the play and, being in a group touring Europe, felt ourselves almost as emissaries of the British people. It was a curious situation that as actors we inflamed each other at the injustice and horror of it. Actors have always been, in the main, idealists and social revolutionaries. Drama is itself a comment on life's flaws and blemishes – not if you're playing in *Dynasty* perhaps, but certainly if you have ever played Ibsen, Shaw, Shakespeare, Brecht, Miller, etc. – the very grist of drama is in the poet's revulsion from iniquity. So, although we weren't all in total agreement, we were a small piece of England touring Europe, and shooting words and not bullets.

> **O, from this time forth,**
> **My thoughts be bloody or be nothing worth.**

The horses have by now taken their places and I join the group. As I do so, Ophelia rises.

SCENE V

How we experimented with Ophelia! We wanted to avoid the pitfalls: the clichés, the wild-eyed stare from a RADA graduate, the sudden darting in, gripping a soiled nightdress as she writhes on the floor – it's all too frequent and familiar. We had to see the madness from her point of view and not make her look dotty. It's too easy and unsympathetic. We must look through her eyes; it is the world that is mad when you are – as in those movies where the camera goes blurry as the actor gets dizzy. So we wished to avoid that nightmare from which most directors seem unable to extricate themselves, seeming to say, 'Oh well, here's that mad scene.' We must make the world mad in Ophelia's eyes.

Ophelia rises and moves down the line of actors who are intoning lines from the play, lines that Hamlet abused her with. All those thoughts that come to nag us – you repeat them as if to glean some new truth from them. So she walks past this wall of voices shouting or whispering and the poor woman's mind is thus made transparent to the audience. So, Sally Bentley moved across the stage, jerked this way and that by the sounds in her head. She moved well and seemed to be caught in a cross-current of air on stage.

These random voices were building up in pace and volume. The taunts of her past . . . *Get thee to a nunnery . . . Where's your father? . . . I loved you once . . . Affection? Pooh!* . . . She twists herself away from these torments but can't escape from torturing her poor mind. The words build louder and the actors rise and move slowly in. She spins like a frightened bird and collapses to the floor. The sounds and words stop. They were only in her mind.

Now, as I remember, the cast were watching her from their chairs like spectators at a madhouse. Gertrude says she will not speak to her. The Gentleman's lines have been given to Horatio and it builds his part and fits in with his character. I am watching from my position upstage. I am not here except in the audience's mind. I need not go off to pretend to the audience that I am in a ship taking me to England. So I watch as if we were but puppets here to strut for a moment or two.

Ophelia sits up. Now the cast is like a group of slightly drunken guests at a dinner party; this must have happened at dinner parties where she became a terrible embarrassment to them all. They watch her as an indulgent, bemused group. They are indifferent to her pain and even find her a source of amusement. Since much time has passed the initial shock of her wounded mind must now give way to boredom

177

and indifference. Her lines are now directed to them. She has become a child trying to amuse the guests. The Queen cannot be bothered.

Queen **I will not speak with her.**

[Horatio]   **She is importunate,**
          Indeed distract, her mood will needs be pitied.

Queen **What would she have?**

[Horatio] **She speaks much of her father, says she hears**
          There's tricks i'th' world, and hems, and beats her
          heart . . .
          'Twere good she were spoken with, for she may strew
          Dangerous conjectures in ill-breeding minds.

I.e. the Queen is talking about her in her presence as with one vague and remote.

Ophelia (*To group*) **Where is the beauteous Majesty of**
          Denmark?

(Hugh guffaws from crowd.) Ophelia has become a child again, trying to perform before a group of uncles and aunts. She has reverted to the escape of childhood and so it is fitting that the group acts like encouraging relatives at a mad tea party. They laugh and giggle at her antics; whisper and nudge each other in the ribs, as if to say, 'Poor old Claudius.' In these ways the chorus reflects her own confusion and creates the situation for the audience and her. She is a child again, entertaining her elders but carrying within her a private hell, which is also expressed in the song she sings. She sings and sometimes the chorus joins in as if it was a popular little ditty of the time, some 'rude' little rhyme in vogue – and perhaps she is changing the words of a popular song to suit her own situation.

Ophelia **. . . God be at your table . . .**

This fitted the idea of the group after supper, stuffed and smoking cigars, feeling drunk and impervious.

Ophelia **'Tomorrow is Saint Valentine's day . . .'**

Here Ophelia becomes enthused and performs her little act, singing and miming the bawdy tale. The audience sings along and encourages her more – just as wickedly insensitive people spur on a nutty person to wild, coarse and abandoned acts.

She sits on the floor and lifts her skirt and pokes her tongue out and generally winds them up while they are still fanning her madness. So what is interesting is not only the victim but the way in which society is part and parcel of the malady. In this case they are linked. After a while the guests become bored. They look disgusted and have had enough. They see how unkempt and filthy she has become. They imagine she stinks and perform lewd gestures to each other. It was interesting to see how the actors threw themselves into this.

Ophelia   **'And thou hadst not come to my bed.'**

Thus encouraged by the guests, Ophelia teases Claudius and sits on his lap – much to screams of laughter at his discomfort. She impersonates a saloon hussy; she pulls him to the centre stage and Claudius, to 'indulge' her madness, allows himself to be used by her, albeit reluctantly. He turns to his guests as if to say, 'Well, what can we do?' Seeing this, she gives him a vicious bite on the leg. Claudius howls in pain and lunges after her but fails to catch her. This provokes even greater hilarity. Humiliated, Claudius signals to the guests to try and catch her. Perhaps this is a new game for them. They hold out their arms to form a circle. She is trapped and can't escape. They surround her and slowly go in, arms stretched out like the leaves of those insect-eating plants, ready to ensnare their prey.

They close in and the circle tightens; and then, as if blessed with that extraordinary power that is given to the mad, she throws them off and the group explodes outwards as if dynamited from within. Now, one at a time, they try to grapple with her, and each one is thrown off and hurled as if she possessed some demoniacal power. She claws, kicks, pushes and sends them flying. Eventually she is subdued by Horatio who grabs her from behind and pinions her ferocious arms within his.

When the King has satisfied himself that her 'fit' has abated he signals to Horatio to release her. Suddenly, as if the current of power that charged her has been switched off, she stands limply waiting.

Claudius   **How long hath she been thus?**

The line is now far more appropriate to the situation.

Ophelia   **I hope all will be well. We must be patient.**

> But I cannot choose but weep to think they would lay
> him i'th' cold ground. My brother shall know of it.
> And so I thank you for your good counsel.
> Come, my coach.

Now Claudius, having accepted her as a lunatic (which, incidentally, renders harmless and senseless anything she might let slip in company), decides to humour her. He whispers some instructions to Horatio to the effect that she should be allowed to act out her fantasy. So, in front of the assembled and bemused faces of the guests, they mime horses! Ophelia whips them with her lash saying,

> Good night, ladies, good night. Sweet ladies, good night,
> good night.

The group enjoys the King's obvious discomfort, and chortles behind their hands.

Claudius **Follow her close; give her good watch . . .**

Thus he relieves himself of any more games and Horatio gallops off with Ophelia in her imaginary chariot. The cast is now stage left, leaving Gertrude and Claudius together.

Claudius **O, this is the poison of deep grief . . .**

During this speech the King wanders up and down stage, growing weaker in his resolve as he sees the place crumble around him. Gertrude by this time has lost interest in the proceedings and, in a vague distracted way, proceeds to take out her lipstick and mirror and repair her make-up. The King is somehow totally isolated from friends or allies and exists in a vacuum with only the ear of Gertrude in which to empty his rotten and somewhat decaying mind. He is a stray satellite without a course or purpose. He desperately needs some guidance and is becoming a pitiable figure. Gertrude doesn't answer him – and in fact says less and less as the play continues. Seeing her absorbed with her lips he smashes the mirror out of her hand. He has gone through his litany of woes and can almost bear no more. Seeing her self-engaged throws him into a fury. I know this goes against his line *O my dear Gertrude*, and so we cut it and left only *Gertrude!* Then he continues:

King   **. . . this,**

180

> **Like to a murd'ring-piece, in many places**
> **Gives me superfluous death!**

Gertrude, put out by the mirror being flung away and by his general behaviour, takes out a cigarette.

From the side we are preparing for the entrance of Laertes. The crowds outside can be heard supporting him with their voices saying, 'Laertes shall be king', over and over again. We hear this through the mouths of the sitting chorus. It starts low, then slowly builds as if he is marching towards the castle with an ever-growing bunch of supporters.

Laertes's entrance.

So the group on the left is now chanting more audibly, 'Laertes shall be king' . . . OVER AND OVER AGAIN. As they say this Laertes rises slowly and begins to walk to his position. Two men rise with him and walk just in front of him, suggesting two guards of the palace. Their arms shoot out, meeting in the middle like metal arms holding the door in place.

> *Queen* **Alack! what noise is this?**
> *King*   **Attend!**
> **Where are my Switzers? Let them guard the door.**

We cut the next speech from the Messenger since it is fairly obvious what is going on, especially as we have gone on chanting 'Laertes shall be king.'

> *Queen* **How cheerfully on the false trail they cry.**
> **O, this is counter, you false Danish dogs.**

Suddenly the Queen, who was saying to Hamlet, *thou hast cleft my heart in twain*, is gunning for Claudius in no uncertain manner and shrieking out like a fishwife how misunderstood they are.

Laertes gets closer to the door – which is the two actors Wolf Kahler and Gary Whelan; their impressive heights and physiques add a menace and weight to their impression of the 'door'. Matthew Scurfield as Claudius starts in my mind to resemble a Mafia villain calling for his henchmen who don't turn up because they know which side to be on when the chips are down. The volume builds. Laertes breaks into a run, but on the spot. He suggests having come from a great distance. He is not as effective as Barry Philips, whose run as 'the Herald' in *Agamemnon* was so spectacular, but it is still good and it works. The drum breaks the movement and voices into a growing crescendo. As Terry McGinity reaches the arm of the door and 'touches' it, the voices will stop as one voice. So, whenever he stops, they will use that as a cue to finish the line on 'king'. 'Laertes shall be king . . . Laertes *King*.'

The drum stops. Laertes puts his hands on the 'door' and suggests its great weight and power by slowly, and with great effort, pushing it open. As it opens slowly, and reinforced by a drum roll, we have the impression of a rebellion forcing its way in. Laertes's hands are holding the wrists of the door/guards, and as he breaks through the guards suddenly take hold of *his* wrists and hold him back. The position is one of a dog straining against two leashes while the stiffened and solid guards hold him back. Laertes is straining forward and the position is still one of aggression and power as his whole body represents attack and energy.

| *Laertes* | O thou vile king, |

Give me my father.

Laertes is straining against the guards holding him, and the veins stand out in his throat like knotted cords as the blood bursts with hatred and revenge.

| *Queen* | **Calmly, good Laertes.** |

Laertes now seizes his cue to demonstrate his self-opinionated tirade on vengeance and the quality of his blood since he is of his parents and therefore true to them. If he was calm he wouldn't be Polonius's son, etc., etc.:

Laertes **That drop of blood that's calm proclaims me bastard,**

Cries cuckold to my father . . . etc. . . . etc. . . .

Somehow one gets used to Laertes mouthing off. We have heard him warn Ophelia that I would sexually exploit her and will be unable to consummate my 'will', being of the throne; and we will hear him gleefully plot with Claudius shortly. In all he is a bag of wind and piss in my opinion – even if Hamlet does have lines later like, *Laertes, a very noble youth* [V, i], I doubt whether Shakespeare was thinking clearly since Laertes's behaviour seems to betray any finer feelings that might have drawn the two together.

So on comes Laertes, puffing away like an express train and blowing his whistle mightily. Nobody much cares . . . but he has the army on his side. This does not seem to be difficult given the quality of Claudius, but does invite the question that if Laertes has the quality to be a king why should his poor sister not have the right to be a princess? Which thought was so condemned by Laertes at the beginning of the play. So here he comes, puffing away, dragging a trail of hyperbole behind him like an old coat.

> *Laertes* How came he dead? I'll not be juggled with.
> To hell, allegiance! Vows to the blackest devil!
> Conscience and grace, to the profoundest pit!
> I dare damnation. To this point I stand,
> That both the worlds I give to negligence,
> Lest come what comes, only I'll be reveng'd
> Most thoroughly for my father.
> *King*   Who shall stay you?
> *Laertes* My will, not all the world's.

Here Laertes breaks away from the guards and leaps on Claudius. They both crash to the floor and the guards crash on top of them. Their jackets fly up and rise over their backs. In a political assassination, or even an attempted one, the assailant is usually pinned to the floor by well-suited security guards. In our case they slid and flopped over the floor like colliding ice-skaters. This particular event seems to make a mockery of the law and order embodied by their smart tailored suits and the actions of thugs. And their jackets always rise up.

They drag Laertes away and haul him on to his feet. The King picks himself up and dusts himself down. One guard holds Laertes by the hair while the other pinions his arm.

> *King*   Good Laertes,
> If you desire to know the certainty

>   Of your dear father, is't writ in your revenge
>   That, swoopstake, you will draw both friend and foe,
>   Winner and loser?
> *Laertes*   None but his enemies.
> *King*   Will you know them then?
> *Laertes*   To his good friends thus wide I'll ope my arms,
>   And . . .
>   Repast them with my blood.
> *King*   Why, now you speak
>   Like a good child and a true gentleman.

Claudius here, with a snap of his imperial fingers, signals to the guards to release Laertes. Feeling confident that Laertes has somewhat burnt himself out, Claudius actually takes Laertes in his arms and Laertes allows himself to be temporarily gathered up. He listens to Claudius's disclaimer.

Ophelia's entrance.

Ophelia is now on one of her walks or fits round the house. Claudius regrets by now that he let the woman have so much freedom and didn't send her off to a loony-bin. But I also imagine that in those days losing your marbles was a pretty common occurrence. She enters and a strange atmosphere enters with her: a thin low hum from the chorus, and Wolf sings very lightly, 'Boys and girls come out to play.' This added a bitter-sweet lustre to it; although it may seem strange in the reading, the effect was most disturbing. In film a composer would have no problem with this idea since it embodies the essence of madness – a retreat into infancy for peace and protection. The musician John Prior added some weird and disturbing sounds on the timpani and piano, and sometimes I noticed that he would use a violin bow against the cymbal. Therefore we have Ophelia enter carrying her atmosphere with her, and again affecting the whole scene as we 'see' it from her point of view.

The chorus's eyes widen and look distracted. The King and Queen drift away. Terry (Laertes) says his lines facing the unseeing eyes of his poor demented sister. He speaks them slowly and carefully, trying to make her comprehend that it is he:

Laertes . . . **O rose of May** . . .

(No answer.)

        Dear maid –

(No answer.)

                kind sister –

(No answer.)

                                sweet Ophelia –

(Same.)

Ophelia sings her song. During this the King and Queen drift back to Ophelia and each takes one of her hands and pretends that it's a rope as Ophelia skips – and all in slow motion.

Ophelia **There's rosemary, that's for remembrance** . . .

She distributes the flowers and we did not pay attention to the value of the flowers in relation to whom she gives them to, except to obey the text and give the correct flowers to the people designated. Each flower has a different meaning and quality, but it will not help the audience to go into each one. Suffice to say that it was a very sad little scene and so delicately and sensitively played by Sally Bentley that as I write this I can see her and am moved by the distance that separates us.

Ophelia imagines that she see the flowers in a field and plucks them from the stage. In this way she carries her dream world with her. It's a far more touching image to me than Ophelia coming on ready with a bunch of plastic prop flowers. She is mad, but liberated. She sings, is bawdy, sad and immune; whereas when she was sane she was harassed, oppressed and victimized. Then she was 'normal'. Now, thank God, she is free of all the utter hypocrisy that goes with civilized behaviour. Isn't that why people go to the theatre? To see passions safely liberated which in life must be choked up and released only on golf courses?

Ophelia finishes her speech and starts to sing. But this time the King and Queen have had enough and try to take her away. She resists and they end up dragging her off to one side. The King forces her into a chair and strikes her, which quietens her down. Meanwhile a distraught Laertes is on his knees. We imagine that this method of calming Ophelia is not unusual in that household.

Laertes breaks down completely and weeps. We tried this in rehearsal – really to cry – since we felt that Shakespeare liberates you and every statement that we make must be taken at full value and not sniffed at. Barry Philips who first played Laertes was reluctant, but in the easy atmosphere of rehearsing with people who have soldiered with you through battles for years, it became easier than he thought. We would always challenge each other to go further and do 'things' that if we found impossible would shed no bad light on anyone. So I said to Barry that if he really loved his sister he might break down and cry. So Barry got on the floor and wept, and it was very moving to see him have a go. To make it easier in the beginning we all got on the floor and cried, and you can imagine that it was a funny sight.

Laertes **Do you see this, O God?**

Laertes is picked up by the King and Queen. He is hauled up like a rag doll. His whole being has collapsed and is being re-formed by the syrup of Claudius who attempts to convince Laertes of his innocence. Laertes speaks through his shaking and crying body:

Laertes **Let this be so . . .**

(Tearful, anguished and totally lacking the aggression he had at the beginning.)

The King now grows in power and, like a vampire, feels renewed strength in the weakening of Laertes who has been demoralized by a second tragedy in the family.

King   **So you shall.**
　　　　And where th'offence is, let the great axe fall.

Here we make some changes in the order of things and follow the tragedy of Ophelia rather than the rip-roaring piracy at sea. We will inform the audience later of 'what happened' to Hamlet through the device of the letter. For now, as if following Ophelia, we make a jump in time. She is dead and we hear gentle bird sounds and picture a sunlit bank at the close of a summer's day . . . we imagine a painting by Burne-Jones of some mossy glade near a stream. I would love to make a film of *Hamlet* for all the visual beauty that is suggested in the text.

Perhaps here I am influenced by the misty image of Ophelia drifting downstream in a garland of flowers in the Olivier film. Of course the text stands up for itself, but as I have already propagated the notion that modern audiences are starved of visual/sensual stimulation, I will add this: life is composed of visual/aural/tactile qualities, and the theatre of Shakespeare tends to operate for too long on one level with the consequent atrophying of the other senses. In Shakespeare's time theatre was simple and uncomplicated since you went to 'hear' a play. Today there are many more levels of human experience that are perceived through the senses, for not only can we actually hear more, we can also see more. Today we demand more rigorous standards and a concept to intrigue and illuminate.

SCENE VII

Ophelia's death.

The sounds of an enchanted wood. From the last scene with Claudius and Laertes we jump to Ophelia's death since we are now following her. We hear bird sounds made by the cast and an atmosphere is created by a bank where a group of children listen to a sad story. We lie on the floor; some cross-legged, as if, at the end of a day at class we are rewarded with some story-telling.

I REMEMBER THIS WHEN AT SCHOOL IN CHRISTIAN STREET, STEPNEY, AND BEFORE I WENT TO WHAT WAS THEN KNOWN AS GRAMMAR SCHOOL. AT THE END OF THE WEEK MISS PARRY WOULD READ TO US *THE HOUND OF THE BASKERVILLES* BY ARTHUR CONAN DOYLE, AND HOW ENCHANTED WE ALL WERE AND HOW WE REMEMBERED FROM WEEK TO WEEK WITHOUT LOSING THE THREAD. THAT WAS THE BEST CLASS OF ALL AND THE ONLY ONE I REMEMBERED. THEN I WOULD GO TO THE PUBLIC BATHS IN BETTS

STREET SINCE WE HAD NO BATHROOM IN OUR PARTICULAR
HOUSE, AND LIE STEAMING IN THE GIANT TUB WITH ITS GREAT
BRASS TAPS, AND THINK OF THIS GREAT HOUND.

So Linda Marlowe became Miss Parry and we children lay at her feet
and lapped up the words like honey:

    Queen   **There is a willow grows askant the brook** . . .

Now, as Gertrude relates this sad story, we actually see Ophelia cross
the stage, and only Sally Bentley with her grace and ballet-trained body
could suggest, while actually moving on her feet, a brook. And as the
speech goes on she starts very slowly to sink, and as she sinks gradually
down Laertes, while listening at the same time, very gently takes her
head as she falls to break her descent. And at the very end of the speech
we see him with the poor drowned Ophelia, as if he had been called out
and seen her there on the bank itself. So when Laertes says,

    Laertes   **Alas, then she is drown'd.**

we see him mourning her, and holding her head with great tenderness.

We now return to the early part of Act IV, scene vii, with the plotting of
Laertes and the King. This is a good rearrangement since we have seen
Ophelia's death and that lends more weight to Laertes's conspiracy.

    Claudius starts with the news of Hamlet coming back. We have last
seen Laertes with Ophelia. The cast now returns to the chairs upstage
and listens.

    King   **I will work him**
        To an exploit, now ripe in my device . . .

And we took this as far as Laertes's *That I might be the organ*. And
then cut the waffle about a Norman called Lamord, which strikes me
as very odd indeed. Let's get down to the meat.

    King   **. . . what would you undertake**
        To show yourself in deed your father's son
        More than in words?

    Laertes   **To cut his throat i'th' church.**

During the following exchange the two actors are positioned facing
each other, profiles to the audience, almost as if they are wrestling;

Claudius's hand on Laertes's shoulders, his body inclined forward. Now the chorus never really sits, but acts almost as a *contre*-audience on stage, either reflecting or guiding the events: a kind of jury. Their faces are set hard during this devilish plotting and they remain still and listening when Claudius comes to the end of his speech:

> King   **If he by chance escape your venom'd stuck,**
> **Our purpose may hold there.**

Matthew Scurfield ends the scene with a diabolical laugh, which starts gradually and builds while Laertes joins in. Eventually the cast is drawn into the laugh . . . which takes them and us to the graveyard as the cast gradually sinks into the stage and makes the most effective 'graves' – all lying there. So, as Hamlet and Horatio walk along the line of bodies, supposedly reading the stones, we come to this empty one being prepared.

ACT V

SCENE I

The bodies are lying as if we see them through their coffins, their hands crossed in prayer over their chests. Horatio and I slowly move across while the laughter fades into that of the one Gravedigger, who turns out to be our one and only ex-Polonius David Auker, singing 'My old man's a dustman, 'e wears a dustman's hat.' Now this caused such a furore from some of our critics that we felt we had come on with our dicks hanging out. The Gravedigger in our many modern-dress productions usually sings an obscure song that in his own time may have been a number-one hit. He would naturally be singing something coarse and simple for the audience since he was, after all, a little bit of pandering to the 'crowd'. Equally today, his song caused a murmur of appreciation since it was unexpected, lively and a welcome provocation to the senses after three damned hours in a theatre. It was a relief. Also it was totally in character. And yet this was picked up by nearly all the critics as something sinful and one of the main causes of our downfall!

So, Horatio and I make our way past the bodies and encounter the one Gravedigger – so we don't need to hear again the two Grave-diggers' pithy aphorisms.

Hamlet **Whose grave's this, sirrah?**

We address the Gravedigger, who remains motionless in his digging position. I shared the lines with Horatio, which not only makes sense but gives Hamlet a low profile, enabling him to observe how society views him, without being observed himself. Usually Horatio stands around like a spare part, smiling at the boss's witticisms. David Auker now plays the Gravedigger with as much relish as he did Polonius. I remember his heavy gnarled hands, which in fact looked like the strong hands of a manual worker.

Hamlet **Let me see.**

(He takes the skull.) Of course it is a mimed skull, since everything else is mimed. He throws it to me and I catch it and make the speech to my empty hand which never looked so full. At the end of this I would throw the skull to Horatio and he would catch it like a ball. We threw it to each other like silly schoolkids playing with death that is so far from them it induces no respect. We then cut to:

Hamlet   **But soft, but soft awhile. Here comes the King . . .**
Now the corpses rise from their graves and become the procession. We hear them first of all. The dirge they sing, which warns us of their coming, is 'Tomorrow is Saint Valentine's Day', which they sing like a funeral march, very sweetly and poignantly. It's most effective and becomes a background for

Laertes   **What ceremony else?**
Ophelia lies there in her nightdress while the others form a line on either side.

Incidentally, the singing of Ophelia's song reminds us of her so vividly that one is almost brought back to the scenes in which she was alive, and it was very moving to see and hear the cast just standing there chanting this as a funeral lament.

Laertes jumps into the grave, which is in fact on the same level as the stage, and takes Ophelia in his arms. He makes his speech, which is rather hyperbolic, and then I come out of the shadows to face him. Now I have my hyperbole:

Hamlet   **What is he whose grief**
        Bears such an emphasis, whose phrase of sorrow
        Conjures the wand'ring stars and makes them stand
        Like wonder-wounded hearts? This is I,
        Hamlet the Dane.
Now I do a 'pretend' leap into the grave. (My voice is getting tired by this time and now must be used at full stretch.) At this stage we are pulled apart, with two men holding me and two Laertes. My arms are pulled back behind me with some force, allowing me to lean forward like a bulldog straining at the leash. Likewise Laertes is held back, and so the two of us are almost nose to nose, ranting at each other; like two savage dogs held back by their masters. This actually has the effect of releasing one's voice since the ribcage is stretched out.

Sometimes great physical effort can have the effect of freeing one's voice since there can be no tension in the throat because all the energy is going elsewhere. Try it.

It's a wonderful speech with its *crocodile* and *mountains . . . Make Ossa like a wart . . .* On this last explosion I go limp, signalling that all my rage is spent. Seeing this, my captors loosen their grip and I quietly and bitterly say,

> **Nay, an thou'lt mouth,**
> **I'll rant as well as thou.**

I leave the scene, uttering quietly for everyone:

> **Let Hercules himself do what he may,**
> **The cat will mew, and dog will have his day.**

Holding Claudius in my eye on the last few words. The company retreats to the seats, leaving Horatio and me together. I cut directly to

SCENE II

> *Hamlet* **But I am very sorry, good Horatio,**
> **That to Laertes I forgot myself . . .**

I have put the scene that usually follows about his escape from the ship earlier on in the play where Claudius says, *Hamlet comes back* [IV, vii] – but in recent times we cut it. So now we are into:

> *Hamlet* **But sure the bravery of his grief did put me**
> **Into a tow'ring passion.**

Osric now comes on, played by Roy McArthur; and, while it is necessary to convey the wager, we trimmed the scene somewhat since it is verbose and bears little value today. Sometimes I believe we are burdened with the legend of some plays that makes tampering with them an act of indecency. Not so in another language. Recently in Vienna I saw a production of *Hamlet* which was totally clear to the audience. The Germans are naturally not bound to translate obscure text but can make a fresh translation for each generation. The benefits of this are obvious. They do not carry forward ancient and

195

confusing text but can suit the words to the age. Though I knew the play well enough to follow it I could not follow all the German, and yet it seemed vibrantly clear. One moment I did understand, and I felt it even improved on the original, or was at least as good: when Hamlet replies to his mother who has asked him to sit by her in the players' scene, he answers . . . *Hier ist ein Magnet mehr stark* . . . for *Here's metal more attractive.* 'A magnet more strong' seemed a very pointed way of describing his affection for Ophelia. Shakespeare really does translate very well into German.

Osric.

I remember that this scene was a pain in the arse. It was well written for the time and was a good parody of verbal poseurs, but these are the scenes that will wear the least well. Of course the scenes built around the passions and philosophy, doubt and confusion and all the tumult of emotion are without compare and suffer no loss with time; but the contemporary scenes can wilt away the greatest patience. So we got on with it and did the right sounds and 'sent up' Osric. All the stuff with the hat is such a yawn now, but it is effective if you have never seen *Hamlet* before.

I liked it when Osric departs and I am left alone with Horatio. The cast are all seated and it is quiet and the play is now sliding towards its end. No more banter from this moment. I have cut until Horatio says, *You will lose, my lord* – leave out the nonsense after Osric has left. I am happy to have reached this summit and can glide softly and swiftly down to death; and that is written in every word and every scene – a kind of farewell in each phrase. We know that Hamlet is reaching towards his end, and this valediction is etched everywhere.

> Hamlet   **Thou wouldst not think how ill all's here about my heart; but it is no matter . . .**
>
> Horatio   **If your mind dislike anything, obey it.**

What a thing to say! Burn it in your heart: *If your mind dislike anything, obey it.* We who are beset with a world of dislikes and turn this poison that we absorb into neurosis. We who are afraid to obey the dictates of our mind, and throw ourselves into a moribund life rather than risk any confrontation.

Hamlet   **Not a whit, we defy augury. There is a special providence in the fall of a sparrow. If it be now, 'tis not to come; if it be not to come, it will be now; if it be not now, yet it will come. The readiness is all.**

This was my preparation for my sacrifice of self; my final words in a sense to Horatio. And they were meant to be a farewell. I looked at Gary and said the words slowly and deliberately, letting them slip – almost bleed – out of me . . . slowly, *yet* . . . *it* . . . *will* . . . *come* . . . *The readiness is all*. I stared at Gary and felt a great emotional surge in me. He was such a loyal partner, and the actor departs from one at such a moment. I was leaving Gary. His large hands seemed never so strong and supportive, and I remembered him in my kitchen spending hours going over what was obvious to anybody and most of all me . . . but 'me' had to deal with everything – or that was my excuse for being hopeless with the damned nunnery scene while Gary would paraphrase it to remind me what it was about. So I looked at his intense and quizzical face and rolled the words out, as if they were mere sops to stop the bleeding; or the crying. There is a way of speaking when you can hold a pause and fill it with an intense passion. Nothing else and no other word will do: passion. To speak too quickly denies it. I imagine such times to be the most intimate that men can ever get together, since the rational world denies too much of this. The most loving – on stage! If you have that emotional power, charge, energy – or call it what you will – you may speak slowly and it will be as if a time bomb is going off inside you.

The scene reshapes itself just as your mind does in typing as you translate feelings into words. The mind begins to order itself and develop a sense of readiness. Without work there is generally a vague undertow of unease, as if a horse was riderless and not knowing where to go. As you order it, other forces way down in the chain of command ready themselves to be passed forward as ammunition. And the more demands that are made, the deeper and deeper go the commands until the whole unit is ready and prepared. The more complex the demands of the warfare the more possibilities are brought into play. They have to be intuitive and adaptable arts to counteract formidable opponents.

The audience is an opponent whose collective mind contains every possibility of human thought. One can win most, but seldom all; a few casualties will fall by the wayside. Only by stretching the audience's imagination to its fullest can one hope to entrap the enemy: by working on the vulnerable underbelly of the audience, its emotions and then its *insatiable hunger* for visual stimulation, and then, finally, the words themselves. These are the three arms of your power. The words are enough – on the radio, that is. How often we are assailed by just one of these elements! 'Let the play speak for itself', as we watch the wooden parade of actors go on and do their thing. It is the English method of warfare. We send the armies out to march into the cannon. And curiously this is the method of theatre: we bore ourselves and others into stultification and lose the battle with the audience who kills us with neglect. The theatre is no longer the 'temple', in George Devine's word, but a toilet.

The duel scene.

Music . . . and John Prior creates the atmosphere while the cast reassembles and freezes into a new position. Terry McGinity, being the third and last Laertes, is the clearest in my mind's eye. I make my speech with relief since it is the last big one, and for that reason I find that my voice has reserves I hadn't suspected – or else it has made a recovery after the graveyard scene. I feel calm and somewhat elated. I have taken from Osric one glove which I place on my hand and am putting on as I speak. The chairs are now at a slight angle to the audience – the first time they have materially changed for some time. They are almost on a diagonal, which allows us to fence on a diagonal and not flatly, left and right. The King and Queen look pleased with themselves. I make my speech and let the words ring out as if I was a showman. It is for everyone I am making this speech.

Hamlet   **Was't Hamlet wrong'd Laertes? Never Hamlet.**

> **If Hamlet from himself be ta'en away,**
> **And when he's not himself does wrong Laertes,**
> **Then Hamlet does it not, Hamlet denies it.**
> **Who does it then? His madness. If't be so,**
> **Hamlet is of the faction that is wrong'd;**
> **His madness is poor Hamlet's enemy.**

Well, that's my excuse anyway. I make it with a show of bravura and *élan*. I am going to show off my fencing skills since I claim I have not been out of practice. But this speech disclaiming responsibility seems very odd. 'Not guilty while the balance of his mind was disturbed.' Is this genuine – this confession to Laertes? Or is he still playing the antic disposition for the sake of the King? No; it's a way of camouflaging his intentions by giving a sop to Laertes. I can't, as Hamlet, go through the long explanations of the Ghost, etc., etc., so let my behaviour at least be apologized for. One day I will tell all; but not now.

Terry faces me and takes himself very seriously indeed as Laertes; as well he should, since he buries himself into a part up to the hilt. It is his way of escaping from himself into the ordered certainty of the play. It's a marvellous ability to sail yourself through the storm: you are cared for every evening at 8 p.m. and you know where you are going and, if you are lucky, you will be loved, or at least admired. Also you have to come to terms with your fears.

I wait for his reply which is couched sombrely while he too is putting on the glove for the foil. I call impertinently for the foils. After all this tongue-wagging let's have some foil-wagging. Laertes calls:

Laertes   **Come, one for me.**

Which then is the set-up cue for Hamlet:

Hamlet   **I'll be your foil, Laertes. In mine ignorance**
> **Your skill shall like a star i'th' darkest night**
> **Stick fiery off indeed.**

Laertes   **You mock me, sir.**

Hamlet   **No, by this hand.**

The King, rightly getting rather bored by all this 'precious' toing and froing, says, 'Let's get on with the bloody thing' – or rather:

    King **Give them the foils, young Osric . . .**

Or they might have gone on all night. Now we choose the foils while Claudius covers up with some banter.

Now, this is the 'bit' the audience has suffered a lot of dialogue to get to . . . THE FIGHT . . . the eventual *coup de théâtre* when the roof falls in . . .

    Hamlet **Your Grace has laid the odds o'th' weaker side.**

A lot of pussy-footing is going on here. Claudius, Hamlet well knows, has horribly murdered his father, and Hamlet is making polite chat to the murderer and staging exhibition bouts! *Your Grace*, indeed!

Now when I called for the foils I mimed taking one from Osric, as did Laertes. With our gloved hand each held and tested the weight and sweep of the blade, and we placed our bodies in the classic position of expert duellists. We would stage the most exciting duel in theatrical history with ne'er a blade in sight! This was an exciting challenge to us and the audience. How tired we were of the blade under the armpit, or the tentative fencing of two novices afraid of committing serious injury on each other.

It happened purely by accident that we came across this most marvellous of inventions. The audience would invent the steel and they would see it slash across the face of Laertes and hear the dancing blades, courtesy of John Prior's percussion. When our first Laertes, Barry Philips, and I worked on the duel we wanted it to be the best of staged fights and we worked endless hours to get it right. But as was natural in learning moves, I would be late with the riposte, or he would, and it became frustrating even as it was improving all the while; and there was still the danger of scooping an eye out as one became more ambitious. John Prior would follow our beats with his drum and add thereby a tempo and dramatic underlining. On one such day my hand was exhausted with all the repetitions, and I said to Barry, 'Let's just rehearse all the moves, etc., without the foil – left, right, parry, thrust, disengage.' We did it to the beat of the drum marking our moves. Suddenly my arm was free and we started to improvise on the drum and to our own inclinations; and it was a discovery. By keeping a careful eye on each other's hand we could react perfectly and appropriately. Eureka: we would have our perfect duel with no foils. I was liberated to swing my 'foil' at great speeds and let it fly through the air as I 'knocked' his out of his hand and 'caught' it to return the other blade to him. It was a fascinating excursion into the magic qualities not only of mime but of suggestion. One had to be not only agile and quick but able to replace the weight of the épée with one's own stance. The climax of the play: the duel to the death, the poisoned blade – and all with nothing to see. Would we be laughed at by the audience as we looked perhaps to them like kids in a playground?

And yet we managed to horrify in a way we never dreamed would be possible. Once the audience became used to us and heard the taps of the drum, they 'saw' the blades whistling dangerously through the air. They would also see the exchange of blades and finally the moment when I ran through the King which would cause the audience to let out a sickening gasp. I love killing people on stage since you can painlessly vent all your fury.

King **Set me the stoups of wine upon that table.**
Matthew Scurfield begins what for him also is his last speech, and that too is weighed by the reserve one has left over if one has husbanded one's energy well. There, with his shiny, bony skull which shines under the light like a full moon, scarred with craters and the canals that make up the map of the cranium, he booms his last triumphant mouthings. He then drops the 'union' or precious ring into the cup, but since the cup is real the ring is mimed and I had to persuade this actor not to make a 'plop' sound as he drops it in since it got a laugh on the wrong thing.

Now the reason why some things are mimed – like the foils and the 'union' and the letters – and others are real – like the glove for the foil and the cup for the drink: there is an absolute reason for this and results from what I feel is vital to us. My miming of the foils did not merely relieve us of the trouble of dealing with the fight; it actually released a power and an ability that would have been quite unavailable with them, unless we had trick foils and the skills of Douglas Fairbanks. We actually improved on the real thing. We *acted* the foils. But we needed real cups to be there because, unlike the foils, they make their appearance discontinuously. We needed to see them since they cannot be used, i.e. played with to release their purpose, like a sword or a mimed ball. The cup is static. The letters that Polonius carries in to the King, on the other hand, are mimed since they are read, and David Auker – another fiendish laughaholic – made great play with the 'unrolling' of these mimed scrolls. I leave it to one's imagination what can be done with them while still making the sense utterly clear. So it is a question of a decision which is dealt with quite quickly at rehearsal. We rehearse with it, and if it gets in our way or in the way of our inventiveness we scrub it. We don't have a designer for whom these props meant many hours of arduous work. I believe that hours of labour should be recognized in something far more worthwhile. I used a real recorder in the scene with Rosencrantz and Guildenstern since I used it to prod them with; but naturally we mimed the horses at the beginning of the second half.

Shakespeare had problems with props. While he wrote, *Think when we talk of horses that you see them / Printing their proud hoofs i' the receiving earth*, at the same time he puts the 'awkward' action offstage. In *Macbeth* the murderers wait for their victims, Banquo and Fleance, who conveniently have to walk for a while before mounting their horses: *So all men do, from hence to the palace gate / Make it their walk.* And even in *Richard III* the problem is made into a virtue by having Richard call for a horse since there was no chance of ever suggesting one on stage or of bringing one on to him. So poor Richard was not in the best place to demand a horse. Murders are also awkward things to stage and should be done offstage. It is the reaction to the horror that convinces us, more than the event. It is the cry of Oedipus offstage that is more horrible than a bungling fake attempt onstage. This follows the Sophoclean tradition where awful events happen offstage and the messenger conveys the monstrosity, since words are always real, whereas amateurish bunglings are disgusting and fake since they come from a desire to horrify through vulgar representation rather than through art and language. I believe the putting out of Gloucester's eyes on stage to be a piece of vulgar Jacobean interpolation, or that Shakespeare was influenced by the box office. But even if it were not, it seems to allow the moronic directors of our time to play with their toy props and horrify in the best video-nasty tradition. I remember the clever Open Theater from New York staging *Arden of Feversham* at the Royal Court in the sixties. They castrated their victim by placing over his genitals two eggs which one of the torturers broke. Horrible image that will stay in my mind for ever.

Conclusion: metaphor and imagination are the poetic renderings of the real event. Impersonations of such horrors belong to the shamateurs who unfortunately populate our conformist theatres.

The King concludes his speech.

We begin to fence – carefully at first, like a ballet. I am offered the drink with the poison and I decline. I fence again. The Queen offers me her handkerchief. I go to her. She sounds like a nagging mother worrying about her little boy. Perhaps the original actor sweated a lot and Shakespeare wrote that line in for future performances since it would be unbecoming for Hamlet to carry a napkin. The Queen then *carouses to thy fortune, Hamlet*. The King in utter horror watches it happen, disbelieving, as in a slow motion nightmare – so we close-up on the action and go very slowly at this point. The music changes and I walk in slow motion until we hear the words:

Hamlet **Come, for the third, Laertes. You do but dally.**

The fencing becomes more frenzied, but still utterly controlled. On the third pass, as I am turning to face him, he slashes me with the poisoned tip. I feel it tear across my arm. We freeze the action. It crawls at snail's pace and I look at my arm where tiny gouts of blood are imagining themselves into being. John Prior actually creates the sound of blood dripping on to the floor: a small, soft percussion sound which, together with my focusing on it and the entire cast freezing, creates the impression of a close-up on it. I feel the whole audience watching my life drip away!

We all go into the slow motion again, and I express shock, horror and amazement. The entire cast moves as if through glue. Laertes looks worried and sick for what he has done. As if from a deep sleep I see my mother's face watching me but looking wan . . . Claudius is watching me with a kind of pleasure . . .

I rip myself out of that time after seeing the blood dripping from my arm, and charge into Laertes fighting furiously. We circle, and by now I am slashing wildly at him; we clash; I lift the sword out of his hand with my mimed foil and catch it with my free hand. (Was ever anything so easy?) He comes towards the sword but I hold him off with mine. I examine the tip – ugly, sharp and gleaming; I throw my sword back to him. Now I shall give him a taste – but he runs from me and is mortally afraid. He expresses terrible cowardice. I chase him round the room and it turns into a farce: he leaps over the chair, but head first like a cat, and rolls on to his feet. I am on him again and whip the sword across his face. I see in my mind's eye a flag of red begin to spread over his cheek . . . someone shouts:

Osric   **Look to the Queen there, ho!**

I turn and see the Queen who seems vague and disorientated. Everything seems to be happening at once and the slowness comes back like a drug; and now I am feeling the effect of the poison. Horatio asks how I am but my eyes are now on the Queen who seems ready to collapse. I shout out:

Hamlet   **How does the Queen?**

The King answers lamely:

King   **She swoons to see them bleed.**

We are in slow time again and every action is thus intensified and blown up. She does not have to rush but can calmly tell me:

Queen   **No, no, the drink, the drink! O my dear Hamlet!**
The drink, the drink! I am poison'd!

– and all this just oozing slowly out and not smudged into the turmoil and the pace of things. Slowly, even as she dies, we have all the time in the world.

But how she dies – in such pain; as the poison starts to eat away at her vitals and she revolts from the iniquity of it all and screams. She sits bolt upright and lets out the most blood-curdling scream I have ever heard. We prepare ourselves for it nightly for it rings in our ears for seconds after, and no matter how far you are away from her – and I can see even now Wolf Kahler's eyes beginning to squint in preparation for the agony to come as that sound eats into your very brain. It is the primal scream of a wounded and dying animal, and it is also the scream of outrage. No one here will die an ordinary death and quietly slip from view. We show what dying and killing are – nothing must be left to chance and smudged over. We will show everything; but it is not the horror of blood and gore but the horror in the *reaction* of the actor. It must be in the pain and agony of the actor that we will appreciate the horror of the murder.

Hamlet   **O villainy! Ho! Let the door be lock'd.**
         Treachery! Seek it out.

A nice juicy line to let rip out your throat, extending the *out* like a threatening, blood-curdling shout, promising in its fury – the ultimate in violence once it is found out.

The whole company moves a couple of paces towards the King as if to trap him. It is as if one released two frames of a film and then froze it. The intention is clear and Claudius already looks trapped so, on the way, we again freeze the action in order to isolate Laertes's speech fully. Laertes is in a state of near-collapse and confesses the evil plot. I listen to his story with horror and the realization that I am not merely wounded but ready for the catacombs:

Hamlet   **The point envenom'd too! Then, venom, to thy**
         work.

At last completely uninhibited by any bonds of restraint, no analysis needed here. I look at the point of the sword; then at the wilting Laertes – a more deadly intent to *Then, venom, to thy work*. The cast completes the seizing of the King and drags him forward like a half-drowned dog, wretched and soaked in his own sweaty fear. I stand there facing him, and with all the time in the world.

I varied the method of killing him. My favourite was to appear to look for the best spot to stab him and bring the sword right up to him as he watched it in utter horror. The audience at this point went very quiet since we were again using our mimed magic weapons. They took part in this almost unwillingly. Their minds were willy-nilly involved since we used no weapons; they were forced to make the weapons in their minds which was more horrifying than anything real on stage. A real weapon would cause them to disassociate themselves momentarily from the play. Shakespeare instinctively knew this. He knew that a sword thrust under the armpit is the fakiest thing, but drinking a potion has a greater credibility since one can actually drink normally as an everyday habit but one is not stabbed to death every day. So, I took the foil and gave it a little thrust into the stomach of the King: a little movement, like you might give to a billiard cue, just to get a hook on him so to speak. He reacts . . . and that is what acting is all about . . . RE-acting. His stomach withdraws as the steel penetrates. My hatred is so pure now, it pours through the steel. The audience are as quiet as death and are really seeing this. I, having 'fixed' him, now ram it in deeper, using the heel of my hand to thrust it in deeper . . . and deeper. Matthew Scurfield equally imagines this tongue of steel threading its way through his internal organs, slicing through. He roars like a bull and the steel is through the body and peeking out the other side. I pull it out with difficulty since I imagine I have gone through some muscle or bone. The cast seizes more tightly on his writhing body. In order to ease out the sword, I place my foot on his chest and pull. It might be a most resistant garden weed. The audience have reacted quite audibly as I thrust in, and now there is a shriek of disgusted laughter as they share this vision with us . . . and 'Oh no's let out, almost as a reflex action audible as I yank the sword out. It makes it gratuitous for the King to say:

King **O yet defend me, friends. I am but hurt.**
So we cut it after *friends*.

    Hamlet **Here, thou incestuous, murderous, damned Dane,**
               Drink off this potion. Is thy union here?
               Follow my mother.

If what I have already been doing with the sword is only enough to badly wound him there is nevertheless a kind of poetic justice in thrusting the poison down his throat, which I do for good measure. I stand back and now let Matthew react to this double treatment he's been having. It takes about four fully grown strong men to subdue him as the combined effects of the poison and the wounding take place. He's held down and suddenly he throws his whole body outward like a spring, and then hurls himself in the air like some demented puppet. Eventually and spectacularly dead, he is dragged to the chair where he is thrown down. To kill a fully grown man is not easy, and one must show the full horror of it.

Laertes now asks forgiveness and, as he makes his valedictory speech, I take off my fencing glove as if all is over and I too fall on my knees. I tell Horatio that I am dying and grapple with him as he tries to take the cup. I cut the first speech and go straight to:

Hamlet **O, I die, Horatio.**
The potent poison quite o'ercrows my spirit.

I cannot get out the slightly purple passage, beautiful as it is, *If thou didst ever hold me in thy heart*, etc. . . . but go straight to:

I cannot live to hear the news from England,

Claudius is at the receiving end of two feet of steel and doesn't look too pleased, though Rory Edwards on the far right is cool about the killing and no doubt waiting for his pint.

> But I do prophesy the election lights
> On Fortinbras. He has my dying voice.
> > . . . the rest is silence.

I take a long time to say the last three words; a long time to take my leave of Gary who now is holding me so gently. I look up at his stern earnest face. He didn't have a huge part but it grew far larger in our production and he relished every second he was on stage and didn't waste a moment or throw a moment away. It was truly Horatio who was holding me. He was my ally all through from the very beginning to the end, since Hamlet must have that relationship on stage.

> *Horatio* Now cracks a noble heart. Good night, sweet prince,
> And flights of angels sing thee to thy rest.

During this we hear the drumming of the approaching army which is made by the now-seated actors stamping in time with their feet. Wolf Kahler now takes the role of Fortinbras. This seems appropriate. He strides on with a marching arrogant, Prussian-like step which, though nothing like a goose step, still evokes some military bearing and dignity. Certainly he does not just walk on. It is an impressive moment and the height and bearing that Wolf has naturally suit the role.

> *Fortinbras* Where is this sight?
> *Horatio*   What is it you would see?

Horatio now lets me down and I view the rest of the play from this position, pretending to be dead while he says his last words. Wolf delivers the rest of Fortinbras most heroically:

> *Fortinbras*   Let four captains
> Bear Hamlet like a soldier to the stage,
> For he was likely, had he been put on,
> To have proved most royal; and for his passage,
> The soldier's music and the rite of war
> Speak loudly for him.
> Take up the bodies. Such a sight as this
> Becomes the field, but here shows much amiss.
> Go, bid the soldiers shoot.

The stamping continues as Fortinbras makes his way off, and all the 'dead' bodies pick themselves up and return to their chairs. We have finished the performance. We sit calmly and relaxed, but still; purged of our duties to the play and the audience. A low wind sound emanates from our throats.

Slow fade in five seconds on lights. House lights up.

Group shot of our small but dynamic company, which captures a serious quality in our faces . . . but if only my shirt fitted me better!
Back row: Bob Hornery, John Prior, Chloë Salaman, Wolf Kahler, Barry Philips, Gary Whelan, Rory Edwards.
Front row: Matthew Scurfield, Linda Marlowe and the author.